Winning Grants

ALA Neal-Schuman purchases fund advocacy, awareness, and accreditation programs for library professionals worldwide.

Winning Grants

A How-To-Do-It Manual for Librarians®

Second Edition

Stephanie K. Gerding and Pamela H. MacKellar
Foreword by Susan Hildreth

Neal-Schuman

An imprint of the American Library Association

CHICAGO 2017

© 2017 by the American Library Association

Extensive effort has gone into ensuring the reliability of the information in this book; however, the publisher makes no warranty, express or implied, with respect to the material contained herein.

ISBN: 978-0-8389-1473-1 (paper)

Library of Congress Cataloging-in-Publication Data

Names: MacKellar, Pamela H., author. | Gerding, Stephanie K., author.
Title: Winning grants : a how-to-do-it manual for librarians / Stephanie K. Gerding, Pamela H. MacKellar.
Description: Second edition. | Chicago : ALA Neal-Schuman, an imprint of the American Library Association, 2017. | Includes bibliographical references and index.
Identifiers: LCCN 2016025285 | ISBN 9780838914731 (pbk. : alk. paper)
Subjects: LCSH: Proposal writing in library science—United States—Handbooks, manuals, etc. | Proposal writing for grants—United States—Handbooks, manuals, etc. | Library fund raising—United States—Handbooks, manuals, etc. | Proposal writing in library science—United States—Case studies.
Classification: LCC Z683.2.U6 M33 2016 | DDC 025.1/1—dc23 LC record available at https://lccn.loc.gov/2016025285

Cover design by Alejandra Diaz. Images © Rawpixel/Shutterstock, Inc. Text composed in Minion Pro and Interstate typefaces.

♾ This paper meets the requirements of ANSI/NISO Z39.48–1992 (Permanence of Paper).

Printed in the United States of America
21 20 19 18 17   5 4 3 2 1

*This book is dedicated to librarians everywhere
who do the hard work of meeting the needs of people in their communities.
This is the core of librarianship and the reason for winning grants.*

Contents

Part I: The Grant Process Cycle

Contents

Part II: Library Grant Success Stories

Part III: Worksheets, Checklists, and Forms

Supplementary materials can be found at **www.alaeditions.org/webextras.**

Figures

Foreword

I am honored to have the opportunity to provide the foreword for this exciting publication, *Winning Grants: A How-To-Do-It Manual for Librarians*. During my career, I have been involved in the full spectrum of grant activities, from preparation to review and final funding decisions. This publication serves as a highly effective road map in the journey of developing a successful grant proposal.

The world of fundraising, particularly pursuing grants, can be daunting. Yet these alternative sources of revenue are critical for the success of our twenty-first-century libraries. Although library funding has stabilized somewhat since the Great Recession of the late 2000s, public revenue is always at risk and we know that economic busts and booms will continue to occur, particularly as the global nature of our economy becomes more and more pervasive. Having a diverse revenue base for our libraries is a wise protection against changing funding situations.

Libraries cannot rely on grants for stable funding, but grant funding can often support the creation of an innovative service program or the development of a new facility that will ultimately create enhanced services and an ongoing revenue stream for the library. Grants can provide the venture capital that libraries can use to move from providing traditional services to serving as the key convener in their communities.

I know many library staff are hard-pressed to find the time to focus on grants since they are busy putting out the fires of everyday public service management. But I would encourage you to try to find the time. The initial effort does not have to be a detailed or complicated proposal. Start small, possibly with a local community or family foundation. Pick a project that is feasible and can make a difference in your community. Identify a small team of people who are interested in the effort. Consider including volunteers or those in your community who may have grant-writing skills and are willing to contribute those skills to the success of the library. Then get started with this publication, as it will provide you with an excellent approach to the grant development process.

Don't be disappointed if your first attempt is not successful. Get back into the game again! I have found that once you've planned for a new service, program, or facility, you will be able to revise and submit new proposals to other funders. Also, if community members are involved in this process, they become very excited about this opportunity and often bring together new or different funders than the ones you initially had considered. Be flexible and ready to take advantage of a variety of funding opportunities.

Collective impact is a common theme among funders today. It is a framework to tackle deeply entrenched and complex social problems. It is an innovative and structured approach to making collaboration work across government and business entities, philanthropic and nonprofit organizations, and individual citizens to achieve significant and lasting social change. Libraries can play a key role in this collective impact work. Librarians are the conveners in our communities and can bring together many parties that are all trying to address challenging problems but need a unifying entity or platform to bring them all together. In prioritizing grant opportunities, I would strongly encourage you to consider partnerships with other public service providers to demonstrate that librarians are leveraging the investment of public funds in a variety of sectors to make a difference in their communities.

I am delighted that *Winning Grants: A How-To-Do-It Manual for Librarians* will be available for our library community. This manual provides great advice for every step in the grant process and the worksheets, checklists, and forms are amazing. Best of luck on your grant proposals!

—SUSAN HILDRETH

◇◇◇◇◇◇◇◇◇◇◇◇◇◇◇◇

Susan Hildreth is currently the Inaugural Gates-funded Professor of Practice at the University of Washington Information School. She also serves as an Aspen Fellow in the Communications and Society Program advancing the work of the Dialogue on the Future of Public Libraries. Formerly, Susan Hildreth was the Executive Director of Peninsula Library System, Pacific Library Partnership, and the Califa Group in California. She served as the director of the Institute of Museum and Library Services, a presidentially appointed, Senate-confirmed position, from January 2011 through January 2015. Hildreth is the former city librarian of Seattle, Washington, where she managed the Seattle Public Library. Prior to Seattle, Hildreth was the state librarian of California, appointed by California Governor Arnold Schwarzenegger. She also served as the city librarian of the San Francisco Public Library and in other leadership positions in California public libraries. She began her career as a branch librarian in the Edison Township (New Jersey) Public Library system. Hildreth graduated cum laude from Syracuse University and holds a master's degree in library science from the State University of New York at Albany as well as a master's degree in business from Rutgers University in New Brunswick, New Jersey.

Preface

When the previous edition of *Winning Grants* was published, our nation was facing the worst economic crisis since the Great Depression. Library budgets were being cut across the board, and librarians had to devise ways to fund programs and services that communities needed more than ever. Librarians have worked hard in these difficult economic times, and thankfully most libraries are surviving and achieving success. Some states and regions have enjoyed an economic recovery in recent years, whereas others have been slow to rebound. Some areas in our country are currently in an economic decline due to falling energy prices, and there are predictions that the nation could be headed for another recession. We cannot predict the future, but it is safe to say that librarians should not count on increased funding in the foreseeable future. It is more important than ever for librarians to master the skill of grant work and build it into their everyday jobs.

There is also more to gain from grant work than a boost to the library budget. Grants can make a huge difference in a library's ability to meet identified community needs, build strong community partnerships, establish new connections, and increase the sustainability of the library itself. Winning a grant is a great accomplishment, and people want to be associated with successful operations. Even small grants can be worth the effort, as they may be easier to obtain and may better fit the scope and intent of a library project. A small grant can also be a good way to test out an innovative service. Many library staff find that one grant leads to others and, thus, results in increased support from community officials.

Where can library staff charged with writing grant proposals under time and economic pressures turn for help? Library schools do not normally offer courses in grantsmanship, and it's rare for a book on grants to take a library-centric approach. This updated edition of *Winning Grants* aims to keep you current and help you hone your grant skills. We designed *Winning Grants: A How-To-Do-It Manual for Librarians* as a one-stop tool with both how-to advice and successful examples that can help anyone associated with library grant work. *Winning Grants* is written in easy-to-understand language with helpful advice that you can apply immediately. Inside you will find worksheets, examples, checklists, and an easy-to-follow, step-by-step Grant Process Cycle—all intended to help you prepare a winning proposal.

Applying for a grant can seem overwhelming and difficult. Librarians and information professionals are often surprised to learn that they possess many of the skills necessary to successfully win grants. They already have the ability to research, synthesize, package, and summarize information; a commitment to reach out, assess community needs, and find solutions; and a cooperative, collaborative professional attitude. This manual provides the necessary tools to create a well-written proposal that describes a worthwhile project planned to benefit your community.

Purpose and Audience

Winning Grants is for anyone interested in learning about grants and writing proposals to fund all types of library programs and projects. Our knowledge stems from experience in every aspect of grant work—as grant writers, grant evaluators, and grant project managers. We have worked for library nonprofits, universities, school libraries, public and special libraries, and state library agencies and have received grant funding from both government and private sources. We present workshops online and around the world and consult with libraries, and we have found that our process works for all types and sizes of libraries. *Winning Grants* provides a step-by-step Grant Process Cycle you can follow that will not only save you time and energy but also bring you success in getting the grants you and your communities want and need.

Good Luck and Have Fun!

We know that grant work can seem intimidating, and our hope is that *Winning Grants* will help your library as you create successful proposals and generate new sources of grant funding for your initiatives. We also hope the grants process will become less a mystery and more an enjoyable adventure. Your journey may include a little trepidation, but remember that writing a successful grant is achievable. Our Grant Process Cycle is easy to follow and will set you up for success.

Librarians have distinct advantages in the grant process: we know how to research, attract partners and collaborators, and discover our community needs, and we have a wealth of creative ideas for serving our users and furthering the pursuit of knowledge. By showing the passion you have for your work in the context of a grant proposal, you are sure to find success.

Grant projects come in all shapes and sizes, in all kinds of libraries, serving diverse communities. With inspiration from others and by using the worksheets and checklists provided, you will be well prepared to seek grants for your own library's projects. There will be nothing holding you back, no reason to hesitate. We wish you the very best of luck! Please let us know about your successes at winninglibrarygrants@gmail.com. We would love to hear from you. Don't forget to visit our *Library Grants* blog (http://librarygrants.blogspot.com) for new library grant opportunities and ALA's Web Extras page (www.alaeditions.org/webextras) for worksheets, checklists, and forms you can use.

Acknowledgments

STEPHANIE GERDING

Much appreciation goes to the librarians who contributed their grant success stories for this book. They are such an inspiration and will be aspiring to new grant writers. Thank you to my sweet husband, Patrick, who cheers me on and brightens my every day. And to my daughter, Madeline, for many reading parties and cups of tea.

◇◇◇◇◇◇◇◇◇◇◇◇◇◇◇◇

PAMELA MACKELLAR

Thank you to my husband, Bruce, who supports me in what I do.

Introduction

Winning Grants is unique from other grant books because the focus is on libraries and on the use of strategic planning and goal setting as the foundation of grant work. This not only simplifies the work involved but also ensures that your efforts directly support your library's larger mission and vision and the actual needs of the community.

The material is arranged in three parts. Part I, "The Grant Process Cycle," features eight chapters that cover the five phases of the Grant Process Cycle. Easy-to-follow examples demonstrate successful implementation. Part II, "Library Grant Success Stories," features real-life success stories that demonstrate the process in practice and provide motivational tips from successful library staff. Part III includes helpful tools, such as checklists, forms, and worksheets, for you to copy and incorporate into your own grant work.

Part I, "The Grant Process Cycle," which details the grant process in eight chapters, begins with chapter 1, "Understanding the Grant Process." This chapter explains the phases of the Grant Process Cycle by outlining the steps necessary to successfully obtain grants. This chapter also provides an overview of the commitments that must be made by a library that is seeking grant funds. Grants are not just free money. Acquiring them requires planning, resources, accountability, and sustainability. Grants involve more than bringing in money; they establish valuable partnerships, resolve community needs, and increase community support.

Chapter 2, "Planning for Success," covers the basics of strategic planning and demonstrates why it is essential to have a strategic plan and community involvement in place before beginning grant work. We help your library get started by showing you how to review your library's mission, priorities, goals, and objectives as stated in the plan. We furnish a sample plan from Premiere Community Library, the fictitious library we use to depict our process throughout the book. This chapter stresses the importance of assessing and prioritizing community needs prior to strategic planning and reinforces the idea that the purpose of grant work is to meet community needs.

Chapter 3, "Discovering and Designing the Grant Project," covers one of the most creative and enjoyable parts of the process—developing the grant project. By developing worthwhile projects that implement your strategic plan and solve community needs, you can prove to funders why you should receive a grant. We explain different teams and their roles in the grant process and the importance of partners and collaborators. We show you how to develop project ideas and goals, outcomes, objectives, action steps, timelines, budgets, and evaluation plans. The included worksheets will be invaluable when it is time to begin writing your grant proposal.

Chapter 4, "Finding Library Funders," explores how to find a funder for your grant project. It covers the different kinds of funding sources—private and government—and includes information about many resources where you can find grant opportunities specifically geared toward libraries.

Chapter 5, "Researching and Selecting the Right Grant Opportunity," shows you how to research grant opportunities in private and government resources. You will learn how to assess and identify those organizations whose purpose most closely matches your library project's goals. An example Keyword Selection Worksheet shows how you can use your project plan's goals and objectives as a starting point to increase your search results, and the Funder Summary Worksheet in part III will help you keep your research findings organized. The section Top Resources for Finding Grant Opportunities, as well as the Winning Grants Sources and Resources Handout in part III, will help you as you do your research. Included in this chapter are research tips and information about how to stay current on grant announcements.

Chapter 6, "Creating and Submitting the Winning Proposal," integrates all your planning and research into the actual writing of the grant proposal. Many applications request the same basic structure and elements—cover letter, table of contents, proposal summary or abstract, organizational overview, statement of needs, project description, timeline, budget, evaluation, and appendix. We explain these components and provide planning and proposal templates (in part III) that allow you to easily adapt, modify, and replicate content for not just one grant but multiple grants, saving you time and money. We also cover how to tell the story of your target audience and grant concept. We provide checklists to ensure that you have a thorough and clear proposal that could make the difference between a winning proposal and a rejection letter.

Chapter 7, "Getting Funded and Implementing the Project," explains what happens after you send off your grant proposal and what to do next, whether your proposal was accepted or rejected. We include discussion of the most common reasons grants are turned down, details on customary grant report requirements, and first steps for implementing your project.

Chapter 8, "Reviewing and Continuing the Process," helps you evaluate your experience with the grant process and improve for the next grant. Repeating the cycle will be easier as your experience grows and you learn from your previous attempts. We include questions to facilitate a review session and ways to keep your grant skills up-to-date through professional development and other collaborative opportunities. We stress the importance of keeping your strategic plan, community assessment, and proposal components up-to-date. By building grant work into your job, you will be prepared to apply for the next grant opportunity that comes along. We also offer eleven Tips for Grant Success to help improve your potential for winning grants.

Part II, "Library Grant Success Stories," includes six real-life examples of grant projects that were funded. If you need a little help with brainstorming creative ideas for your project or want to get advice from other librarians who have completed grant projects, check out these inspiring success stories from libraries around the country. These selections include best practices and offer you a chance to see how successful programs have been developed, funded, and implemented. There is nothing like a "real-life story" to give you inspiration, spark some grant project ideas, illustrate successful partnerships, demonstrate innovative programs, provide best practices, and teach you about what pitfalls to avoid.

Part III, "Worksheets, Checklists, and Forms," contains valuable tools that you can copy and use as you work through the grant process. These tools are also available as Microsoft Word documents and PDFs at www.alaeditions.org/webextras. This enables you to complete the forms with your own information and share the materials with your teams. The following resources will help you stay on track, keep you organized, and take you through the Grant Process Cycle, starting with your library goals and finishing with a successful grant proposal:

- Making the Commitment: A Checklist for Committing to Library Grant Work
- Library Planning Checklist
- Grant Partnership Agreement Worksheet
- Strategic Plan Worksheet
- Project Planning Worksheet
- Project Action Steps Worksheet
- Project Timeline Worksheet
- Personnel Budget Worksheet
- Nonpersonnel Budget Worksheet
- Project Budget Worksheet
- Evaluation Plan Worksheet
- Keyword Selection Worksheet
- Funder Summary Worksheet
- Winning Grants Sources and Resources Handout
- Questions for Funders Checklist
- Grant Proposal Worksheet
- Grant Submission Checklist
- Debrief and Review Checklist

Following part III, this manual ends with a glossary full of useful library grant terms as well as a bibliography of resources mentioned in the book and additional ones for further reading and study.

Part I

The Grant Process Cycle

Understanding the Grant Process

Successful grant work is the result of planning, organizational capacity, fulfillment of community needs, sustainability, relationship building, and evaluation. Grants are not free money that will magically solve your library's budget problems. This book covers proposal writing and grant research but also focuses on the planning process necessary to have a successful project and a justly awarded grant. Grant work is a holistic process that must include all facets of the library's planning and as much staff and community involvement as possible. It is also a rational process based on project management principles. We will cover the entire grant process and help you develop core grant proposal components that are useful for all grant applications.

We provide examples along the way to show you the concepts in action and practically applied. In part III, you will find blank worksheets you can copy and use as you go through this process in your library. The part II stories from real libraries where grant projects were successfully implemented reveal some important tips and practical advice you can use. These real-life examples will help you envision innovative and successful grant projects and gain advice from other librarians who have effectively completed the grant process. This selection of best practices offers you a chance to see how award-winning programs have been developed, funded, and implemented while providing a great view of the big picture of the grant process.

IN THIS CHAPTER
- ✓ Phases of the Grant Process Cycle
- ✓ Making the Commitment
- ✓ Gathering Knowledge

Phases of the Grant Process Cycle

In this book, we have divided the grant process into five easy-to-understand phases. Visualizing the grant process in sections or phases will make it easier for you to understand and approach this kind of work. Breaking down the process into smaller phases also makes it easier to explain to others. Many people avoid grant work because they think it is too difficult or too complicated. This is usually because they misunderstand the nature of grant work and what it involves. There is a misconception that applying for grants is one huge monstrous job that you have to take on all at once. You may think you will need to drop everything else to apply for a grant. This could not be further from the truth. As you will find out in this book, grant work is an ongoing

Plan for Success

Implement, Evaluate, Continue

THE GRANT PROCESS CYCLE

Design Winning Grant Projects

Create the Winning Proposal

Research Funders and Grant Opportunities

process that takes place in phases across a span of time and involves many activities you are probably already doing. When you follow this process, you will be ready with the information you need when it is time to apply for a grant.

Phase 1: Plan for Success

Throughout the grant process, we encourage you to refer constantly to your library's strategic plan. If your library doesn't have a plan, make it a priority to develop a planning process before applying for grants. If this isn't possible, your library should at least have a written mission statement that can be used as a basis for project development decisions. A strategic plan provides the framework that is needed for the grant process to be effective. Having a plan in place will help prevent mission creep—or creating poorly designed or unneeded projects for your library only because grant funding is available. If you develop every grant project from the goals and objectives in your library's plan, this will eliminate the possibility of creating projects or programs that aren't relevant to your library's mission or your community's needs. A plan also answers many of the questions that are found in the requests for proposals (RFPs) that charitable organizations rely on to determine their grant awards. A library with a strategic plan is a more dependable and organized applicant. A plan demonstrates to a funder that fund money will be used responsibly and not wasted on a hastily developed new idea.

Your library must also know the compelling issues in your community before applying for grants. Discover the true needs of your community and what will make your library's efforts meaningful and important. This will be very helpful when you begin to develop your project ideas and when you demonstrate need in a grant proposal. Chapter 2 covers the importance of strategic planning and methods for needs assessments in more detail, including a sample strategic plan for the Premiere Community Library, the fictitious library we use to demonstrate our process throughout the book.

Phase 2: Design Winning Grant Projects

Chapter 3 covers a step-by-step method for developing grant projects. This is often one of the most creative and enjoyable parts of grant work. Every project should be a worthwhile solution to a community need identified in the planning process. Whether you want to build a new library or create a program for teens, your project design consists of the actual activities you will perform based on your library's plan. Project planning teams discover and design viable projects that fulfill a need in your community. This team may include representatives from library leadership, community advisors, partners, staff members, and subject matter experts. The size of your project planning team will correlate with the size of your library. Large libraries may have project planning teams that focus on designing projects to meet specific needs.

Projects are the implementation arm of your strategic plan and should be designed before beginning to research funders and grant opportunities. The slickness or length of an application is seldom a critical factor in determining who will receive a grant. Rather, it is the project that counts. And when projects are based on community needs, funders can understand the reasons why the project is important and relevant for funding. If funders can't determine why you are developing a project, they will not be willing to support it. We show you how to plan your project by developing goals, objectives, outcomes, action steps, timelines, budgets, and evaluation plans. The project planning worksheets in part III will be invaluable when it is time to begin writing your grant proposal (see pp. 170–194).

Phase 3: Research Funders and Grant Opportunities

Once you have a project design, you may realize that the library does not have adequate funding. This is when your project turns into a grant project and you decide to look for grants to fund the project. Chapter 4 explains how to locate applicable and viable grant funders for your specific project. It covers the two major types of funding sources (government and private), including where to find current library funding opportunities in both online and print formats. Selecting the right grant necessitates knowing what a funder is interested in supporting and knowing how closely the funder's mission matches the purpose of your project.

Once you know where to find grant opportunities, you are ready to do the research and select the right grant. This step of the cycle, covered in chapter 5, is often a straightforward one for librarians as it involves something librarians are experienced at doing—research. Learn how to increase your search results with the Keyword Selection Worksheet (see part III, p. 182) that uses your strategic plan's goals and objectives as a starting point. Keep your research findings organized with the Funder Summary Worksheet (see part III, p. 183). Our *Library Grants blog (http://librarygrants.blogspot .com) is a helpful free website to use in your research.*

Phase 4: Create the Winning Proposal

Once you reach this part of the grant cycle, your planning work will be complete and writing the proposal will involve refining your ideas into the stipulations requested by the funders. Chapter 6 guides you through creating a proposal using the plans and information you already have compiled. Most grant proposals have the same basic structure and requirements. The common components are these: cover letter, table of contents, proposal summary or abstract, organizational overview, statement of needs, project description, timeline, budget, evaluation, and appendix. Some parts of the proposal are narrative and involve telling the story of the grant project and the people it will serve. We provide checklists to ensure you have a thorough and clear proposal that could make the difference between a winning proposal and a rejection letter.

Forming a grant team will help minimize the workload while increasing the likelihood of success. If you are working in a small library, you can still have a team, especially with the addition of community volunteers. We explain the qualities necessary for an ideal grant writer. Some libraries are reluctant to apply for grants due to the misconception that they have no employee with the necessary skills. You may be surprised to find that many of the needed abilities are ones that are developed in everyday library work. Library staff excel at many of the skills necessary for grant work. Librarians who are adept at researching, connecting with the community, creating justifiable and well-planned projects, and effectively writing and communicating can be successful with the grant process. Grant work is really about four things librarians are great at doing:

- Conducting research
- Answering questions
- Building relationships
- Serving the community

We also cover the responsibilities and skills of all team members, including the grant coordinator, and how to successfully organize grant team meetings.

Phase 5: Implement, Evaluate, and Continue

Chapters 7 and 8 cover what happens when your project gets funded, implementing your project, evaluating the success of your project, and continuing the process. It may be weeks or months before you receive notification that your grant application has been accepted. The funder may contact you with questions or requests for more information. Whether your proposal was accepted or rejected, you need to know what to do next. Included in this chapter is an explanation of the most common reasons grant proposals are turned down. If your project gets funded, the implementation process begins. You will need to revisit your timeline and budget and make any appropriate updates. Project management is an important aspect of implementing a grant project. We include details on customary grant report requirements. Don't forget to celebrate this great accomplishment with the entire grant team and library.

Grant work is an ongoing process, so the cycle should be repeated. This is the time to look back and then move forward with the knowledge you've learned from your first completion of the Grant Process Cycle. Facilitate a review session with your grant team using our Debrief and Review Checklist (see part III, p. 197) and keep your relationships with partners and funders thriving. Remember to thank funders and follow up with any reporting requirements. Keep in contact with them and let them know how your project is progressing. Many professional development opportunities are related to grants for libraries, so keep up-to-date by attending workshops, subscribing to electronic discussion lists, networking, and researching new opportunities.

Making the Commitment

One important requirement for success with grants demands a strong commitment throughout the entire process from library leadership, staff, and grant coordinators. They must be committed to each step of the process: planning, partnering, research, project development, writing, implementation, evaluation, and follow-up.

This book will give you a firm foundation in understanding the grant process, but your library must be responsible for making the necessary commitments. Can your library really commit to the grant application and implementation process? The library leadership (director, board, trustees) and any staff who will have responsibilities tied to the grant or grant project should be involved in the decisions. Most grants will have benefits, but also obligations, and in some cases maybe even specific constraints or drawbacks that you need to consider. If your project does not fulfill the funder's guidelines, you are wasting your library's time and funds by preparing a hopeless grant application. And, of course, you are also wasting the funder's valuable time. This is not the best way to build a relationship with a potential funder.

There are both advantages and disadvantages to applying for and receiving grants. Sometimes it may not be worth the effort and requirements necessary to apply. There may be too many hoops to jump through, you may not be able to fulfill the stipulations requested in the RFP, or your library may not have the support necessary for implementation. The funding must be worth the time, effort, and resources needed. These resources include not just the staff time spent planning a project and writing a proposal but the time to be spent in implementing and evaluating the project as well.

All grants have costs for the submitting library. Sometimes these are obvious, such as matching funds or staff time, but other considerations include the impact of assigning key staff members to the duration of the project, the building space and supporting materials needed, the time needed for meetings and communication with everyone involved, and the impact of neglecting existing essential activities while focusing on the new project.

Depending on the type of library you work with, applying for a grant may include working with other departments or meeting requirements set by your local authorities, system, or development office. This is especially true in university settings, so make certain you understand the local stipulations that will affect your library's grant work.

Although there are a lot of considerations to weigh, grant money can also make a huge difference in your library's ability to provide service for your community. Even small grants can be worth the effort as they may be easier to obtain and may better fit your project scope and intent. One grants officer said she would love to give huge grants, but sometimes smaller grants are more appropriate for certain projects and libraries.

Numerous small grants are available from local funders, and many have fewer strings attached than do those from larger private or government agencies. You could also apply for several small grants that in combination could provide for all the facets of a larger project.

Ask yourself the following questions before you begin a grant proposal:

- Does the funder have restrictions or requirements that would shape or affect our grant project in an unacceptable or undesirable way?
- Can we continue the project if grant funds are discontinued? What would be the effect on our clients or organization if the project were stopped abruptly?
- Should we propose a new project when we really need money for existing programs?
- Would this project take too much time and attention away from core library programs?
- Is this the right grant for this project?

Specific Commitments

The Grant Process Cycle is ongoing, which means the commitments continue as well. Some of these commitments should be made before the library decides to pursue grant funding. Others cannot be made until you have designed your grant project and researched and selected the appropriate funder's grant. At that time you should revisit these commitments. Your library must be able to commit to accountability, effective

---

FIGURE 1.1

MAKING THE COMMITMENT: A CHECKLIST FOR COMMITTING TO LIBRARY GRANT WORK

The following questions will help you determine if your library can really make the commitment to apply for a grant.

COMMIT TO ACCOUNTABILITY
- ☐ Will the grant project definitely support your library's vision and mission?
- ☐ Will your library leadership support the project?
- ☐ Will the library director commit the necessary resources to the project/grant?
- ☐ Will the library staff have the time needed to complete the application process and to implement the project?
- ☐ Will the grant team have the necessary supplies, equipment, services, and space?
- ☐ Can the library follow through on the agreements made in the grant proposal?
- ☐ Will the library spend the funds as specified and keep accurate accounts?
- ☐ Will you make sure there are not other organizations in your community already doing your project and filling the need?
- ☐ Can all deadlines be met and grant reports be filed on time?

COMMIT TO EFFECTIVE COMMUNICATION
- ☐ Will your proposal be as clear, concise, and honest as possible?
- ☐ Will your goals, objectives, and activities be clearly identified and understandable?
- ☐ Will you be able to convey that your library and the project are important?
- ☐ Will you ask the funder for what you really need?
- ☐ Will all the library staff, board members, leadership, partners, and volunteers be continually informed about the grant?
- ☐ Will you ask the funder if the library's grant project clearly fits the funder's interests?
- ☐ Will you communicate with all your contacts?

COMMIT TO MEETING COMMUNITY NEEDS
- ☐ Will your library identify the needs of your community?
- ☐ Will your analysis include enough information to educate and inspire the funder?
- ☐ Can statistics be used to quantify the problems identified?
- ☐ Can you use stories and cases regarding specific patrons or programs to illustrate the needs?
- ☐ Will your grant project focus on solutions to meeting community needs?
- ☐ Will you identify a target audience for your grant project and involve representatives in the planning process?

communication, meeting community needs, planning, partnerships, evaluation, sustainability, and following the grant guidelines. The Making the Commitment checklist (see figure 1.1) will help you determine if you are ready and able to make the commitment to doing grant work. This checklist is also available in part III (see p. 165) for you to copy and use in your library as you go through this process. If your library has made these commitments, you are now ready to continue the Grant Process Cycle.

COMMIT TO PLANNING

- ☐ Does your library have a strategic plan? Will you review it before writing your grant?
- ☐ Will you have a project plan that includes goals, objectives, and activities and is based on your strategic plan?
- ☐ Will you set deadlines?
- ☐ Will you organize your materials (research, grant materials, etc.)?
- ☐ Will you have a budgetary goal?
- ☐ Will you have a method to track tasks and contacts?

COMMIT TO PARTNERSHIPS

- ☐ Will you cultivate a strong relationship with your grant funder?
- ☐ Will you develop the appropriate collaborations to leverage resources, share expertise, and support the project?
- ☐ Will you determine what groups in your community share your library's vision and goals and approach them as partners?
- ☐ Will you invite community members to focus groups and planning sessions?
- ☐ Will you complete a partnership agreement outlining goals, responsibilities, and benefits?

COMMIT TO EVALUATION

- ☐ Can your library clearly identify success in respect to the grant project?
- ☐ Will you have an evaluation plan and/or logic model to determine if your project has met its goals?
- ☐ Will you be able to identify what impact your project achieves or what difference the project makes?
- ☐ Will you identify outcomes for the project? Will your project have meaningful results that cause a change in people's behavior, attitudes, skills, condition, or knowledge?
- ☐ Will you have a benchmark plan designed to measure each outcome?

COMMIT TO SUSTAINABILITY

- ☐ Will your project be completed?
- ☐ Will your project be supported by leadership after grant funds are depleted?
- ☐ Will you plan a funding strategy to continue your project after grant funds are depleted?
- ☐ Does your project involve more than just one person?
- ☐ If your project involves hiring new staff members, will their positions be maintained after the grant period ends?

COMMIT TO FOLLOWING THE GRANT GUIDELINES

- ☐ Will you check and double-check all instructions?
- ☐ Will you answer all questions and complete any required narrative sections?
- ☐ Will you compile all allowable attachments, including letters of support?
- ☐ Will you obtain all the required signatures?
- ☐ Will you submit the grant on time?

Gathering Knowledge

Hopefully, this long list of commitments hasn't made grant work seem too daunting. It is a process, and once you've gone through it the first time, it really does get easier. If you are a novice to grant work, here are some tips for finding out more about the process:

- Ask other librarians to share their grant proposals. (See the part II success stories, pp. 141–161.)
- Become a grant reviewer or talk to grant reviewers. This is a great way to find out how difficult it can be to give money away! You will learn exactly how grant decisions are made, which can help you immensely.
- Contact your state library for help. Some state libraries offer free classes, and consultants often know which libraries in the state are expert grant seekers that you could contact for advice. Many state libraries also provide grants to libraries through LSTA (Library Services and Technology Act) funding and state grants-in-aid.
- Find out if potential grant funders will share successful proposals. Not all funders will do this, but it is worth asking. Many funders' websites list the organizations they have funded in the past and may also showcase successful grants.
- Tell everyone about your grant project ideas and get input. You never know who may know of a good lead or what opportunities may develop.
- Talk to the leaders in your community to find out about local grant funding.
- Contact other nonprofits and community organizations in your area. Do they know of funders? Are they applying for grants? Are they looking for partners?
- Discover the professional development opportunities available in your area. Foundations will often offer seminars for free or low cost. Some online educational sources are covered in chapter 8.

Once you complete the Grant Process Cycle, you may find that you have achieved more than you had expected. There are often additional benefits beyond the grant funds. If you follow the guidelines in this book, you will increase community support and find new partners and collaboration opportunities. You may even see an increase in the library's local budget and an increase in library use.

Planning for Success

The Grant Process Cycle emphasizes planning because plans are the foundation upon which you will write your grant proposals. Plans provide the framework for project development, and they include many of the core elements required in grant applications. Libraries with strategic plans are prepared to submit grant proposals without a great deal of extra work. Librarians can more easily identify appropriate grant opportunities for their projects when they know what they plan to accomplish and where they need additional funding. For these reasons, libraries with plans can respond to RFPs quickly and without much lead time. Strategic planning is about being proactive rather than reactive. Libraries with plans do not respond to RFPs by inventing projects to match them. Libraries driven by their purpose are focused on securing grants to make a difference for people.

This chapter and the next focus on planning. Chapter 2 stresses the importance of community assessments and strategic planning as the foundation for your library's grant work. Chapter 3 takes you to the next step of planning and designing your specific grant project. The focus of a strategic plan (chapter 2) is usually on the entire organization, while the focus of a project plan (chapter 3) is typically on a particular service, program, or project. Both types of planning are linked, and they are both essential to successful grant proposals. You must know what you do and why you do it. Essentially, this means you first need to know your library's mission and vision, its purpose, and the true needs of your community. Then you can establish how you are going to meet those needs.

Planning Is Essential for Success with Grants

Strategic planning requires understanding your community's needs, and it demonstrates that you have designed library programs, services, and projects to meet those needs. Libraries with plans have much greater prospects for a successful future, and they are able to contribute to their communities' biggest aspirations. Libraries with plans will have more success with grants because that is what funders are striving for as well. A strategic plan is your compass. If you ignore your strategic plan, you may soon find

Plan for Success

Implement, Evaluate, Continue

THE GRANT PROCESS CYCLE

Design Winning Grant Projects

Create the Winning Proposal

Research Funders and Grant Opportunities

that your mission "creeps"—or shifts—due to external factors such as the lure of money or outside influences. When a library loses its way, staff do irrelevant work and they may apply for grants that don't relate to the library's plan or mission. This is a recipe for failure with grants.

For example, if your library's plan and mission promote advancing literacy, it makes sense to seek funding for literacy projects. You have already determined that there is a significant need for literacy classes in your community. If you submit a grant application to fund a project to teach auto mechanics because you saw that a grant is available for teaching auto mechanics, this is a sign that you have ignored your plan and forgotten your mission. Implementing a project that doesn't relate to your community's needs is a waste of time, money, and effort. If a community's greatest need is increased literacy rates, applying for grants to hire literacy tutors or purchase homework resources would be a better match for your library. By applying for the wrong grant, you have effectively shifted your purpose to fit the guidelines of the funder rather than the needs of your community. Don't do this. Funders can usually tell from your grant application if you wrote a grant proposal to fit their priorities rather than focusing on your community's needs. Proposals that do not demonstrate how you will meet a real need are usually unsuccessful.

Grant funds go to the libraries that are successful and organized. These libraries have strategic plans, they create programs that are needed and efficient, they operate their organizations professionally, and they succeed at their missions. (See figure 2.2, Library Planning Checklist, on p. 31; it is also included in part III on p. 167 and online at www.alaeditions.org/webextras.) This is what any funder/investor wants. This is also what people in the community desire—that the library address their particular needs in the best possible way.

Strategic planning has been encouraged in libraries for several decades, and today most librarians understand the importance of planning. Planning facilitates funding, encourages partnerships, and establishes direction for libraries. Many government and nonprofit funders require a plan as part of their grant applications. Most public libraries must have strategic plans to be eligible for LSTA grants from their state library agencies. Academic, school, and special librarians understand that strategic planning aligns their libraries with their larger organizations, invites collaboration, and maximizes limited funds. Librarians have learned that strategic planning helps them to work more effectively and efficiently to meet people's real needs. Staff benefit from plans because they understand what they are doing and why. The results are clear. Not too long ago there were few library strategic plan examples to follow; however, today a Google search for "library strategic plan" yields many examples from all library types and sizes.

Your library may not have a strategic plan. Possibly you don't have any control over the fact that your library doesn't have a strategic plan. Don't feel hopeless. It is still possible for you to write grant proposals. If your director has given you the job of writing grant proposals and your library doesn't have a plan, we want to reassure you. You can use needs assessments and plans developed by other organizations. Often you will find that large nonprofits in your area have already done a needs assessment that might be viable. Cities, counties, universities, or school districts in your region may have plans already completed that you can use.

Basics of Strategic Planning

Strategic planning is a powerful tool used to guide a library to improve, to prioritize, to ensure that all staff members are working toward the same goals, and to assess and adjust the library's course in response to changing situations. Strategic planning is a deliberate effort to determine the appropriate decisions and actions that will shape and guide what a library is, what it does, and why it does what it does. Planning helps guide the future, establish new partnerships, form creative and innovative relationships between stakeholders, and, ultimately, better address the needs of your community.

A strategic plan should be dynamic, constantly updated to reflect changes in the library and community. Once developed, it should not be imprinted with gold leaf and placed in a safe. When a major change occurs or an improvement is needed, you must revisit and update the plan. Major changes may include planning for a new or remodeled building or creating a new political arrangement, such as combining city libraries into a county system or dealing with budget cuts. Major shifts in populations or demographics due to large influxes of immigrants will surely change the community's needs. Strategic planning stresses the importance of making decisions that will ensure the library's ability to successfully respond to changes in the environment and the needs of the population.

Throughout your strategic planning process, it is vitally important that all library staff and community representatives become involved. A community-wide strategic planning process will benefit from the wisdom of a diverse array of participants and ensure greater likelihood of success. While it is important to involve the community in the library's planning, it is also very important for the library to be involved in any community or organizational planning and to support those plans. Libraries that are active participants in their communities', universities', schools', or corporations' planning will find partners and support for their own plans.

We've talked to librarians all over the United States and are always amazed at the passion they have for their jobs and how they love contributing to their communities. Many have a vision of the ideal library—a place they envision as the perfect setting for their libraries—a place where they and others can do their best work. If staff members are involved with the planning process, they can contribute their energies toward reaching that dream. The result will be staff who feel ownership and joy in their jobs. Likewise, if the community is truly involved in building its dream library, the library will become a true center of the community.

You need a planning committee. At the very least include the library director, library board, staff, and community representatives. If possible, invite governing officials, library volunteers, and patrons to public planning meetings. In a small library, strategic planning might take place as part of quarterly or monthly board and staff meetings; with a larger library, the planning committee might make progress reports to the board and meet more frequently. The committee should have representatives of all your community's demographic and socioeconomic groups from all parts of your service area. Think about including members of your chamber of commerce, local government officials, school districts, churches, and social service agencies.

Start by focusing on the library's vision and mission. Then identify the key background information on your community and library. Next, conduct a needs assessment to determine community needs, how well your library is serving your community, and what improvements you can make in terms of services and programs. Finally, establish goals to work toward the vision and accomplish the mission, objectives to achieve the goals, and specific activities that will be the implementation part of the plan. The goals, objectives, and activities in your strategic plan will determine which projects you develop as well as what grant opportunities to seek and pursue.

The Premiere Community Library's strategic plan (see figure 2.1 at the end of this chapter) is an example of a two-year, goal-based plan. Most plans range from two to three years. Any further into the future and it becomes increasingly difficult to incorporate imminent changes in the library's infrastructure, community, technology, and so forth. Plans vary in length; some are succinct, four to eight pages in length, while others are considerably longer and more detailed.

Assessing and Prioritizing Community Needs

You cannot create a strategic plan that meets community needs without first determining what those needs are. Start by clarifying the meaning of "community" for your library. "Community" consists of all the people the library serves; therefore, community needs are the needs of all the people the library serves, not just the needs of the people who use the library—for example, all the people who live in a city, village, or town; all students, staff, faculty, and researchers in a college or university; all students, teachers, administrators, and staff in a school or postsecondary institution; all employees, medical staff, patients, and their families in a hospital; or all lawyers, legal assistants, and staff in a law office. Community is not limited to library users but includes everyone the library serves, users and nonusers alike.

A community needs assessment examines and analyzes the needs of all the people in your community. Identifying the needs and issues of your community is an essential part of the information-gathering process prior to planning. It is not acceptable to conclude that you "know" what your community needs because you have lived there for a long time or you have worked at your library for decades. You may be confident that the community loves the library, and you may think you know what they want in a library because you regularly talk with users about their satisfaction. Ask yourself whom you are calling the "community." Is it just the people who come to the library and tell you what a great job you are doing? What about the people who have never been to the library? What do they need? Why don't they use the library? Could it be because the library does not meet their needs?

How do you assess what your community needs? It is important to access your entire community using accepted assessment methods to identify community needs prior to strategic planning. You must get input from all segments of your community, not just the politicians, leaders, and people who use the library, but also the farmers, teens, recent immigrants, and all large groups in your community, including people who don't use the library. Everyone has information needs. Is the library serving the whole community?

One common misunderstanding among librarians is to confuse community needs assessments with customer satisfaction surveys. Customer satisfaction surveys find out

BENEFITS OF STRATEGIC PLANNING

1. Creates a clear definition of the library's purpose, which leads to efficiency and effectiveness

2. Provides a clear blueprint for the future

3. Informs staff and management to facilitate clear decision making that is responsible and productive

4. Produces a commonality of vision and mission that bridges staff and library leadership

5. Increases staff morale and job satisfaction through their being informed partners

6. Determines the library's priorities to the community based on the greatest needs

7. Establishes realistic goals and objectives consistent with the mission

8. Provides a basis for ongoing evaluation, measurement of progress, and informed improvement

9. Ensures the most effective use of the library's resources (staff, budget, etc.)

10. Strengthens responsible accountability to governing authorities and the public

11. Increases your chances of winning grants

if library users are satisfied, including what they like and don't like about the library, whereas community needs assessments determine what your whole community needs. These are two entirely different measures. Do not waste valuable library resources conducting customer satisfaction surveys to prepare for strategic planning. Your plan must address the entire community, not just library users or people whom you know love the library.

It is also essential to understand the difference between community needs and library needs. Often, when we ask librarians about their communities' needs, they tell us about what their libraries need, such as more money, more staff, a building addition, more materials, updated computers, new furniture, or 3-D printers. You cannot know what the library needs until you know what your community needs. Taking a shortcut by skipping a community needs assessment will take you off course, and it could jeopardize your success with grants. Focusing on what the library needs will not help you win grants. Funders want to know what the community needs, not what the library needs. For a library to be on the right path, staff must know what they are doing to meet community needs.

You must not only determine people's needs and prioritize them but also ascertain the preferences and perceptions of those most affected by your work. Librarians are usually interested specifically in people's information needs, or needs that relate to the library's mission or purpose. Typically, librarians assess people's information needs for the purposes of determining the library's priorities. However, many libraries are serving as community centers, gathering places and recreational or entertainment destination centers, and learning centers. The library's purpose is no longer limited to providing information in the traditional sense.

Focus on finding out how the library can help improve and support your community, whether it is improving literacy, teaching job-seeking skills, offering educational support, reducing school dropout rates, providing a safe place for teens, or offering technology training and support. Community needs assessments serve as a starting point for determining project goals and objectives, and they help you create evaluation plans to measure your progress. It is important to know how well the library is serving its community and what other services or resources you can provide in the future. You can do this only if you understand your community's needs.

What do needs assessments have to do with grants? A needs assessment is necessary to write a grant. The assessment will tell you what you must know to write a needs statement. Needs statements are required in most grant applications as the standard way to explain or prove the necessity of your proposed grant project. You should always determine a need before you create a grant project. Funders want to see real data to "prove" a need, not your personal opinion of what people need. Needs assessments show why your project is necessary, who will benefit from the project, and how they will benefit. Think of the grant project as a solution to meet a need that was revealed in the community needs assessment.

Results of a needs assessment can be used to determine the following:

- How the collections and technologies can be improved to meet community needs
- Who is using the library, who is not, and how to reach nonusers
- What are the most and least desired/needed services and programs

- Where there is a lack of services in the community where the library can help
- How the community is changing
- What staffing and library hours changes are needed to accommodate the community

The first step in performing a needs assessment is to decide who will oversee it and conduct it. Needs assessments can be carried out by outside consultants, library volunteers, or library staff. Your available resources, time frame, and comfort level with performing this type of research can influence your decision. It is best to use a combination of these methods. For example, you might hire an outside consultant to help you set up the needs assessment study and design surveys, but then use volunteers to actually conduct a telephone survey, and staff to interview community leaders. Members of the library board can help with all phases of the community needs assessment.

- *Outside consultants* will have expertise in how to conduct research studies. They provide objectivity by offering an outsider's view. Since consultants are educated and experienced at performing this kind of research, this option makes better use of your limited time. The primary disadvantage to using outside consultants is often the cost.
- *Volunteers* can help with conducting surveys and compiling data. They do not cost money and they save library staff time. However, be aware that they may present a biased interpretation of what the community needs. It is important to select volunteers who reflect a broad array of community members and who have experience in performing needs assessments. Volunteers will also need to be trained and managed, so some staff time will also be involved.
- *Library staff* can also perform needs assessments. While library staff are less expensive than hiring outside consultants, they may be inexperienced in needs assessments or not have time to perform a needs assessment on top of their regular library responsibilities. However, basic needs assessments can be done through interviews and research, as outlined in the following section on collecting data.
- *Library board members* can help to plan and conduct assessments as well as compile and synthesize data. The board's responsibility is to help the library meet the information needs of the community, guided by the library's vision, mission, and plan. It is the job of the library board to perform duties that relate to this purpose. Most library board members want to contribute and make a difference for the community. Assisting with a community needs assessment is a great way to use their talents.

The second step in performing a needs assessment is to decide what you want to learn about your community and what kind of information you plan to collect. For example, will you perform a broad-based study or one that is focused on a particular area or issue? Some categories of information you might be interested in collecting include historical, demographic, economic, social, cultural, educational, and recreational. Your community profile could indicate areas that are lacking or needs that the library could meet. Take a close look at your community's characteristics to show you the way. Some libraries perform a SWOT (strengths, weaknesses, opportunities, and threats) analysis or use another strategic method to identify the challenges and opportunities facing their communities and libraries. Then they prioritize the issues and use the needs assessment to focus on addressing those specific issues.

Collecting the Data

Now that you have decided on the types of information you want to collect about your community, you need to determine how to collect that information. You can collect data by interviewing key leaders in the community, holding a community forum, researching demographic data from public records and reports, and performing surveys. It is best to use more than one of these data collection methods.

Interviews

By interviewing key members of your community, you can better understand their impressions of the community's needs. Interviews may also yield future partners who could support grant projects. However, this method provides subjective data because it is based on opinions that may not reflect the needs of the entire community. If you are interested in a target audience, such as Spanish-speaking members of your community who aren't using the library, you can contact leaders who work with that specific population, such as church officials, health care workers, or teachers. If you have two staff members to assign to this task, they could split up and each conduct five interviews or they could go together so that one could take notes while the other asks the questions. A volunteer could also help with note taking.

Focus Groups

Focus groups can provide very honest and useful information. Members can be selected by age, gender, occupation, or social interests, and groups can be organized into manageable numbers. If the participants are comfortable, they may give very helpful feedback. You will need to have a facilitator for each group, and organizing and scheduling focus groups can take a lot of time. Information gained through focus groups is also subjective, and compiling the data could be time-consuming as well.

Community Forum or Town Meeting

A community forum involves holding a group event and inviting your entire community. This can provide a lot of good information, give visibility to your library, and even raise its status within the community. However, these forums require a lot of planning and publicity. The majority of the attendees will probably be active library users, rather than those who do not use the library. This can make it difficult to determine the needs of the entire community. Another disadvantage of this method is that it tends to provide subjective and impressionistic data about the community's needs. Also, the less vocal and participatory segments of your community may not be represented.

Surveys

Surveys can be distributed by mail or conducted over the phone, in the library, or online. While mailed surveys are the most expensive option and get low response rates, the mailed survey method requires very little time to implement and is easy to coordinate. Some utility companies will include surveys with their bills for no charge, so this is an option to explore for some types of libraries. Several online surveys are available for free or little cost. These are easy to develop, implement, and compile. Take a look at SurveyMonkey (www.surveymonkey.com), Zoomerang (www.zoomerang.com), and Google Forms (https://docs.google.com/forms/u/0/?pli=1); they offer free versions for smaller surveys. Some libraries have links to online surveys available on their websites to gather information from online users.

Information gathered from surveys is only as good as the questions you ask. If you have no experience designing surveys or if you are not confident in this area, you might want to consult an experienced surveyor as you design the questions. The shorter a survey, the easier it will be for a busy community member to complete. Be sure to provide confidentiality to your survey participants. Reassuring your participants that their survey responses will be kept confidential and anonymous might help improve your response rates, especially in a small community.

Using and Sharing Community Feedback

To make use of the information you have collected, the results have to be interpreted and evaluated. When the data analysis is complete, prioritize the responses. At the end of this process, the findings should be compiled and shared with library leadership, staff, and the community. This can be done through meetings, public displays, or articles on your library website or in the local newspapers. Of course, once you have broadcasted these needs, make sure that the library will follow up on the top priorities.

Community needs assessments are not monumental events that you launch every decade or so. You can keep current with your community by regularly holding smaller community feedback groups or periodically conducting focused surveys in your community. Stay current with trends in your community by reading the local paper and attending meetings of local organizations and clubs. Talk with directors of local agencies to get a sense for the trends they are experiencing. When you are constantly assessing community needs and staying on top of trends in your community, you will be prepared to respond quickly to grant opportunities to meet current needs.

Common Plan Elements

Some elements found in most strategic plans are also common in most grant proposals or applications:

- Vision
- Mission
- Community and library profiles
- Goals
- Objectives
- Activities

When you have conducted a community needs assessment and your strategic plan is complete and current, you will already have much of what you need for a grant proposal. Having this information in place gives you an advantage when it comes to responding quickly to RFPs. The example strategic plan for the Premiere Community Library, included at the end of this chapter (see figure 2.1, p. 27), illustrates the previous six elements in a typical strategic plan outline format.

In addition, most grant applications require another element:

- Needs statement

A community needs assessment will provide the information you need to write a compelling needs statement. If you want an effective plan, you must conduct a community needs assessment prior to strategic planning anyway. Although strategic plans don't often include a needs statement as such, plans are a direct reflection of community assessment results.

Vision

The vision depicts an ideal library that is instrumental in creating your future community. Vision is the motivating force for your strategic plan. Vision statements are inspiring and easily communicate what drives your library's day-to-day efforts. Your vision will tell you what the successful implementation of your strategic plan will look like. Your vision should include the following qualities:

- Exciting
- Provocative—should stretch and challenge your library
- Realistic
- Desired
- Representative of legitimate beliefs
- Described in positive terms
- Written in the present tense, as if already achieved

Vision provides "pull" for organizational practices. This is sometimes called the heliotropic principle. Just as plants grow toward their energy source, communities and organizations move toward what gives them life and energy. Vision allows us to imagine beyond our current circumstances and reach something truly original, not just reactionary. Real vision is a picture of a desired outcome we want to create, not just a dream.

Visioning must be a participatory process. A vision won't be effective if it's handed down from a single library leader or administrator. To achieve a shared community vision, key stakeholders and interested community members must spend time together talking about their ideas and listening to one another. As you incorporate everyone's ideas, the vision is likely to evolve and grow stronger. Indeed, you will increase your community's ownership of the vision and commitment to achieving it. Community involvement engages people and organizations in discovering what empowers libraries when they are most effective.

Try to remain focused on the vision or what you want to create, not problem solving. Problem solving tends to concentrate people on situations we don't want or on what isn't working. Of course, most of us, in both our professional and private lives, spend far more time problem solving and reacting to circumstances rather than focusing our energies on creating what we really value. We can get so caught up in reacting to problems that it is easy to forget what we actually want. Problem solving becomes the busywork of organizations in which people have forgotten their purpose and vision.

Mission

The mission is a broad statement of the role or purpose of the library. It identifies whom the library serves and justifies its existence. All library staff should know the library's mission and be able to connect their specific responsibilities to it. It should inspire their actions and give them an understanding of what the library is working to achieve. The community should be able to understand the library's purpose and the services it offers by reading the mission.

Mission statements are brief but powerful and easy to understand. Some mission statements comprise multiple paragraphs; some contain just one sentence. Mission statements are broad so that they do not need to be rewritten when new initiatives or directions are undertaken. They are free of language that may discourage potential funders or partners from participating. Often funders will evaluate a potential grant recipient by how well its mission statement aligns to their own.

The mission statement answers the following questions:

- What are the basic purposes for which the library exists?
- Whom does the library serve?
- What basic community needs are we meeting and with what services?
- What makes our purpose unique and distinguishes us from others?
- Is our mission in harmony with our community?

If your library is not succeeding at the work of its mission, it may be time to reevaluate the library's work and/or the needs in the community, initiate training, fire underperformers and hire new talent, or more. Foster a culture of mission-based decision

---

EXAMPLE LIBRARY VISION STATEMENTS

- **Dartmouth College Library:** "Inspiring ideas for personal transformation and global impact." (www.dartmouth.edu/~library/home/about/mission.html?mswitch-redir=classic)

- **Lufkin Middle School Library:** "The Lufkin Middle School Library helps all patrons maximize their success in an atmosphere that fosters personal responsibility, values learning, and respects cultural diversity." (http://lufkin.middle.schoolfusion.us/modules/cms/pages.phtml?pageid=245700)

- **Brooklyn Public Library:** "Brooklyn Public Library will be a vital center of knowledge for all, accessible 24 hours a day, and will be a leader in traditional and innovative library services which reflect the diverse and dynamic spirit of the people of Brooklyn." (www.bklynlibrary.org/about/mission-and-vision)

- **LA Law Library:** "LA Law Library is a vibrant community education center in Los Angeles County and a leader in providing public access to legal knowledge, putting national and international sources of law into the hands of those seeking legal information." (www.lalawlibrary.org/index.php/about-us/mission-vision.html)

making (not decision making based on insecurities, limits, unwillingness to try new things, ego, personal agendas, entitlement, etc.).

Community and Library Profiles

You need to look at your environment and truly understand your library and community before you do any planning. Changes in politics, society, and economics constantly impact our libraries. Libraries are in the business of providing information and must respond to the changes in our communities, keeping up with new and different community needs and reaching out to new populations. An analysis of the community will reveal important information that the library director, staff, and board must know, including indications about what the current population needs from the library. A community profile is used to guide the focus of a community needs assessment. Using the profile and assessment, a library can then respond by redefining its mission and roles and reallocating the collection, services, and programs to more accurately match the actual needs. When you start by profiling and assessing your community, you can determine what the people need prior to planning. Then the remaining plan elements will more easily fall into place.

Community Profile

A community profile is a brief description about the population and area the library serves. Your city or state, a university or corporation, or other local organizations may already have completed a community profile. If so, it is fine to use an existing community profile as long as it is current. Community profiles are usually done every three to five years or when you are aware of a major shift in your community.

If you do need to develop your own community profile, you will have to gather specific information about the library's service area and the people it serves. Researching public records and databases collects objective secondary data, such as the social indicators or demographics of your community. The U.S. Census Bureau (www.census.gov), a well-known and reliable source, provides quality data about the nation's people and economy on a county or city level. Explore the website for useful tools to help you, such as American FactFinder (http://factfinder.census.gov/faces/nav/jsf/pages/index.xhtml) and American Community Survey (ACS; www.census.gov/programs-surveys/acs). Through the Census Bureau, you have access to such community information as ages, genders, languages spoken, education levels, income levels, marital statuses, and more.

The community profile will document changes and new trends in people's lifestyles, interests, family and business pursuits, recreational activities, and social, civic, and educational concerns and will help the library reallocate its resources to provide what the community needs and expects. A comparison of historical data could be useful to illustrate any dramatic changes that have taken place in your community, such as unemployment trends or an influx of people from other countries.

This information can reveal major phases in a community's existence, whether it is growth, stagnation due to economic hard times (loss of businesses, jobs, homes),

---

EXAMPLE LIBRARY MISSION STATEMENTS

- **Harvard Library:** "The Harvard Library advances scholarship and teaching by committing itself to the creation, application, preservation and dissemination of knowledge." (http://library.harvard.edu/vision-mission)

- **Topeka & Shawnee County Public Library:** "Your place. Stories you want. Information you need. Connections you seek." (https://tscpl.org/about/mission-statement)

- **Zionsville Community High School Library:** "The library media center will empower students to be critical thinkers, enthusiastic readers, skillful researchers, and ethical users and creators of information through direct instruction with students, collaboration with staff, and a media program that provides a variety of programs, services and resources." (http://cms.zcs.k12.in.us/zhs/?q=node/369)

rebirth because of outside forces (new businesses, new populations), or the need for dramatic change to remain viable and economically strong. The two major influences to be examined are the environment and the population; include analysis of the following:

- Community setting: environment, geography, climate, and recreational opportunities
- Growth and development
- Local government
- Business and industry
- Communications
- Educational facilities
- Cultural opportunities
- Local organizations and civic groups
- Population characteristics (age groups, races and languages, educational levels, occupation and income levels, household sizes)

Library Profile

The library profile is specific to your library. It is a component often requested in a grant application and sometimes called an organizational overview. The library's history, service population, achievements, primary programs, current budget, leadership, board members, and key staff members should all be included. Answer the questions "Who are we?" and "What do we do?"

The library profile should include basic information but can also incorporate recent changes and interesting details about the library on these topics:

- History
- Service population
- Achievements
- Primary services, programs, collections, and facilities
- Current budget and resource reallocations
- Leadership and staff
- Cultural diversity initiatives
- Technology infrastructure
- Collaboration and partnerships
- Proof of significance
- New laws and regulations
- Major achievements

Needs Statement

A needs statement articulates what the people in your community need. It is a combined result of what you discover when you research your community profile and conduct a community needs assessment. Look at the needs your library currently meets and compare those with the community's current needs. Are there any gaps between what your library currently offers and where you want to go to be more effective? If so, decide the new needs you want to address in the time period covered by your plan.

Write a narrative that presents the data demonstrating current community needs and explain why you have chosen to prioritize a few to address in the next few years. This serves as the needs statement for strategic planning purposes. It defines problems and clarifies what is lacking using verifiable facts and real data. A needs statement is not what the library needs; it is what the community needs that the library can address.

Having needs statements for your prioritized needs helps get buy-in and commitment from the community, board, and staff. Needs statements will focus staff on what they are doing and the desired results, and they will ensure the community that you are using resources to help them. When you have a needs statement in place, it will be ready to adapt to any grant application that is a good fit for your library.

Library service responses are used to prioritize library services and programs that match the community needs identified through a visioning process. There are several models of service responses and service priorities. *The New Planning for Results* (2001), by Sandra Nelson with the Public Library Association, is a community-based planning process that defines thirteen service responses meant to help public library planners link community needs with library services and programs by defining the library's role:

1. Basic library
2. Business and career information
3. Commons
4. Community referral
5. Consumer information
6. Cultural awareness
7. Current topics and titles
8. Formal learning support
9. General information
10. Government information
11. Information literacy
12. Lifelong learning
13. Local history and genealogy

Academic libraries, school media centers, public libraries, and special libraries alike can use this list by adapting it to reflect the services/program areas that apply to their communities' needs. If your library fulfills a need not on this list, write it in. The idea is to choose to do a few things very well rather than spreading energy and resources across too many efforts, thus reducing your effectiveness. It is better to meet a few needs of your community than to miss the mark and not help solve any of the community's issues.

Goals

The next step in the strategic planning process is to define goals. Once you have goals, you will be able to develop specific, measurable, achievable, realistic, and time-bound objectives and create activities designed to achieve those objectives. This is all in preparation for designing specific projects that your library plans to implement (see chapter 3).

When you have well-planned projects in place, you already have what you need to respond to appropriate grant opportunities.Goals are the actions you will take to achieve the library's vision. One of the main functions of a strategic plan is to establish clear goals and realistic strategies to achieve those goals. Goals are broad, general statements describing a desired condition or future toward which the library will work. They are the path to achieving the vision of the library and part of the solution toward fulfilling the needs identified in the needs assessment. Set your sights high when it comes to goal setting. Some libraries really only compile a checklist of what they know will be achieved rather than push themselves to go beyond the norm. Push yourself. If a goal is not accomplished, it shouldn't be viewed as a failure; rather, it means that a review should occur, changes may be needed for success, or perhaps it should just be viewed as a learning experience.

Some goals may be short term, while others will cover a multiyear period. Achieving a goal may mean changing the services or programs offered by the library. All goals should be written in positive language. Goals often become the services, programs, or projects that may be supported by grant funding. Goals must be framed in the context of the community served. If a goal is not stated in terms of a community benefit, you should think twice about taking this path.

Objectives

Objectives are written for each goal but may also relate to more than one goal. Objectives are short range and more focused than goals. The acronym SMART—specific, measurable, achievable, realistic, and time-bound—is often used as a way to remember the important elements in writing objectives. Check each objective you write to make certain it meets these conditions. Objectives are the way the library measures its progress toward reaching a goal. For that reason, it must be very clear what the objective will accomplish and how you will measure the success of the objective.

Statements of objectives should include the following:

- A specific, realistic, and achievable end result
- The measure to be used
- The time frame

Activities

Part of the strategic planning process is to develop a series of activities or strategies you can use to reach your goals and objectives. These activities will form the basis for many of the library's actions and resource allocations for the period covered by your overall plan. At this point in strategic planning, you will need to be very specific about what will be done. Sometimes called project planning, this involves detailing everything necessary for effective implementation of the project, including identifying action steps, allocating resources, creating timelines, determining the budget, and establishing evaluation methods. And, of course, as you plan for these activities, you are also building the foundation for possible grant projects. The specifics of grant project planning and evaluation are covered in chapter 3, "Discovering and Designing the Grant Project."

Project planning can be a creative process done by a committee. Brainstorm the activities necessary for accomplishing individual goals and objectives or combinations of goals and objectives from your library's strategic plan. There should be a direct link between your objectives and your activities. You might find that a single activity addresses more than one goal or objective. Also, some activities might help accomplish more than one objective.

Strategic Planning Resources

There are many resources available that will be helpful in implementing a planning process for your library. Some focus on libraries, but there are many others written for nonprofits that librarians will find useful. This chapter and the bibliography section of this book include some helpful recommendations.

If your library does not have a strategic plan, look to your state library agency, library system, or professional organization for guidelines, tutorials, and FAQs (frequently asked questions) about strategic planning. Many also have format suggestions and links to examples available on the Web. For example:

- *Nebraska Library Commission*: http://nlc.nebraska.gov/LibAccred/planning .aspx
- *Massachusetts Library System*: http://guides.masslibsystem.org/ strategicplanning?hs=a
- *Private Law Librarians and Information Professionals*: www.aallnet.org/mm/ Publications/products/Law-Librarians-Making-Information-Work/pll-guide -8.pdf

There are books on strategic planning for school library media centers, such as *Strategic Planning for School Library Media Centers* by Mary Frances Zilonis, Carolyn Markuson, and Mary Beth Fincke (2002) and *Toward a 21st-Century School Library Media Program* edited by Esther Rosenfeld and David V. Loertscher (2007). Sandra Nelson's (2008) *Strategic Planning for Results* provides an excellent community-based planning process for libraries. This type of plan is not limited to public libraries, as every library serves a community, whether it consists of people in a city, town, or village; students, faculty, and staff in a college or university; employees and staff in a corporation; or teachers, administrators, and students in a school. Nelson's method has proven successful with all sizes of libraries as well as with museums, churches, and schools. Nelson's book provides precise details on everything you need to do to create a library plan, including aspects of every meeting and how to help staff respond to change. This process is based on involving a community committee and prioritizing the library's services.

EXAMPLE ACTIVITIES FOR OBJECTIVE 1.1 FROM THE PREMIERE COMMUNITY LIBRARY 2016–2018 STRATEGIC PLAN (see figure 2.1, p. 27)

1. Partner with local ESL teachers
2. Perform assessment of Spanish-speaking community members' needs
3. Collaborate with other local agencies serving the Spanish-speaking population
4. Provide staff with training on cultural awareness, sensitivity, and service
5. Revise current library policies that impact delivery of services for Spanish speakers
6. Hire a bilingual librarian
7. Make website accessible for Spanish speakers
8. Market library to Spanish speakers in the community in their native language
9. Involve Spanish-speaking community members in planning

Monitoring and Updating Your Strategic Plan

Regularly revisit your plans and evaluate whether you are meeting the goals and whether action steps are being implemented. Perhaps the most important indicator of the library's success is positive feedback from the community concerning services, programs, and resources. Having established clearly defined outcomes and outputs will provide a feedback mechanism to evaluate program performance and will influence future planning, resource allocation, and operating decisions. When your plan is current and you are aware of any adjustments you must make or possible funding shortfalls, you will be able to monitor available grants for appropriate opportunities.

While you may have created a strategic plan, you must continue to take into account the trends, emerging issues, and critical events that may impact your plans. Pay attention to outside forces that could sway your strategic goals toward other directions. Sometimes called environmental scanning, this involves finding dynamic connections among the trends and patterns to identify opportunities and challenges. You can do this for your library by using these simple techniques:

- Reading/watching/listening/trying—looking outside of your interests
- Keeping a file of interesting technologies or social changes and recording the patterns that you see
- Paying attention to the current issues in society overall and in the areas of technology, economy, ecology, and politics
- Reading local newspapers and publications to stay in touch with trends in your community, such as changing demographics and emerging health or economic issues
- Discovering opportunities—looking at what is currently happening and the implications those events have for the library's service to the community
- Talking with community members and local agency directors about trends they are seeing—feet on the ground

Some funders require strategic plans as part of the grant application. Funders appreciate strategic plans because good strategic plans achieve the following:

- Show that the library has assessed and prioritized community needs
- Indicate that the library is capable of responsibly handling funds and implementing projects
- Demonstrate that you have given your project idea careful thought, and that it is realistic
- Provide evidence that the library monitors, evaluates, and measures progress toward goals

The professional, polished, and beneficial organizational attributes in the Library Planning Checklist (see figure 2.2, p. 31 in part III) earn confidence in capabilities, raise buy-in, set higher expectations for outcomes and efficiency, and generally engender support. Donors, as with all other community partners in a library's work, support organizations that show potential for excellence. If your library isn't operating professionally, you could lose grant opportunities. When grant donors receive applications from libraries that demonstrate professional best practices *and* also articulate in their grant application that this is how they conduct themselves, these are the libraries whose grant applications will be awarded.

Strategic planning does not happen overnight. It should be a deliberate activity conducted by the library director, staff, board, and community participants. Planning takes time and effort, but it is well worth it simply for the fact that a plan will tell you what you are supposed to be doing and why as well as whom it will benefit and how, and it will align the entire staff toward achieving common goals. In the end, strategic plans are essential for success with grants. If your library doesn't have a strategic plan, how do you even know that you need grant funds? Only because your budget is slim? You should never create new projects for your library just because you need money and a grant is available. The process of obtaining grant funding should directly tie in to your strategic plan. You will find that the main components for grant proposals and the inspiration for grant projects are easily found in a well-developed strategic plan. Just by examining your library's mission statement and vision, you can often gain some essential information that will be helpful when seeking grant funding.

FIGURE 2.1

SAMPLE STRATEGIC PLAN: PREMIERE COMMUNITY LIBRARY 2016-2018

VISION
The Premiere Community Library is the true center of the community. The library responds to the community's essential information needs, informs and inspires the people who use it, and is significant in the lives of everyone who lives here.

MISSION
The Premiere Community Library provides all community members resources, services, and programs in the library and online and offers opportunities to enrich and fulfill their lifelong learning, informational, and leisure needs.

LIBRARY PRIORITIES
With the Premiere Community Library's Vision and Mission statements as a starting point, the Community Planning Committee, made up of members representing the diverse community, established four priorities for library resources, programs, and services that they determined will best meet the needs of the community at this time:

Cultural Awareness
Residents will have programs and services that promote appreciation and understanding of their personal heritage and the heritage of others in the community.

Lifelong Learning
Residents will have the resources, services, and programs they need to explore topics of personal interest and continue to learn throughout their lives.

Informed Decision Making
Residents will have the resources they need to identify and analyze risks, benefits, and alternatives before making decisions that affect their lives.

FIGURE 2.1

SAMPLE STRATEGIC PLAN: PREMIERE COMMUNITY LIBRARY 2016-2018
(continued from previous page)

Information Literacy

Residents will know when they need information to resolve an issue or answer a question and will have the skills to search for, locate, evaluate, and effectively use information to meet their needs.

Goals, Objectives, and Activities

Based on the priorities selected by the Community Planning Committee, the Library Board adopted three goals designed to meet anticipated community needs in the next three years. Each goal has specific objectives and activities designed to achieve those objectives.

Goal 1

The Premiere Community Library's resources and services are culturally sensitive, and they are designed to meet the diverse and changing information needs of the community.

Objective 1.1

By July 2017, provide 50 percent more services and programs to meet the needs of Spanish-speaking community members.

ACTIVITIES

1. Partner with local ESL teachers
2. Perform assessment of Spanish-speaking community members' needs
3. Collaborate with other local agencies serving the Spanish-speaking population
4. Provide staff with training on cultural awareness, sensitivity, and service
5. Revise current library policies that impact delivery of services for Spanish speakers
6. Hire a bilingual librarian
7. Make website accessible for Spanish speakers
8. Market library to Spanish speakers in the community in their native language
9. Involve Spanish-speaking community members in planning

Objective 1.2

By December 2016, provide at least three programs to serve the growing population of refugees from foreign nations.

ACTIVITIES

1. Provide staff with training on cultural awareness, sensitivity, and service
2. Investigate refugees' information needs
3. Involve native speakers as interpreters and library liaisons
4. Perform outreach to these new populations in neighborhoods and schools
5. Revise current library policies that impact delivery of services for this population
6. Provide programs to address their needs in neighborhood locations
7. Partner with other local agencies serving these populations
8. Make website accessible for these populations
9. Market library in their communities and in their languages
10. Involve refugee populations in planning

Objective 1.3

By July 2018, increase by 50 percent the number of programs that bring together multiple diverse populations.

ACTIVITIES

1. Using evaluations from programs for all segments of the population, plan programs to serve the entire community
2. Involve liaisons and representatives from diverse populations in planning
3. Market programs community-wide in multiple languages

Goal 2

The Premiere Community Library serves the lifelong learning, informational, and leisure needs of the community's growing mature adult population.

Objective 2.1

By the end of 2017, at least 40 percent of the adult population aged 55 and older will be registered library users.

ACTIVITIES

1. Conduct a needs assessment to determine lifelong learning, informational, and leisure needs of the mature adult population
2. Assess all possible barriers in the library and on the website for people aged 55 and older
3. Evaluate library's ADA (Americans with Disabilities Act) compliance
4. Conduct promotion with incentives to sign up people aged 55 and older
5. Perform outreach to older adults in assisted-living facilities and those who are homebound
6. Partner with local agencies that serve older adults
7. Spotlight materials in areas of the collection and on the website that are heavily used by older adults
8. Develop collections, provide programs, and offer services with people aged 55 and older in mind

Objective 2.2

By the end of 2017, participation in programs geared toward mature adults will increase by 30 percent.

ACTIVITIES

1. Organize speakers for seminars on health and wellness, retirement, financial and legal issues, relationships and stress in retirement, working in retirement, leisure and volunteer pursuits, Social Security and Medicare
2. Provide computer training that will help older adults find information they need
3. Spotlight library materials relating to programs for older adults
4. Create a page on the library's website with useful information and links for older adults
5. Make programs fun by including music, prizes, opportunities for communicating together, crafts, and so forth

FIGURE 2.1

SAMPLE STRATEGIC PLAN: PREMIERE COMMUNITY LIBRARY 2016-2018
(continued from previous page)

Goal 3
The Premiere Community Library strives to educate the community about the information in the library, how to access it, and the importance of evaluating information prior to making important life decisions.

Objective 3.1
During 2017, the library will increase programming that helps people use technology to access the information they need by 100 percent.

ACTIVITIES

1. Find out what kinds of information people are seeking
2. Reallocate staff time to provide training and plan programming
3. Develop programs designed to meet people's specific information needs, such as Social Security, health information, applying to college, finding a job, homework help, and so forth
4. Provide training on how to find information using the library's website
5. Provide training on how to search the Internet effectively
6. Provide training on evaluating online information
7. Provide instruction on the use of online catalog and research databases

Objective 3.2
By July 2018, 10 percent more community members who were not previous library users will indicate that the library met their information needs.

ACTIVITIES

1. Perform outreach activities geared toward nonlibrary users
2. Actively seek and respond to collection development suggestions from the community at large
3. Find out what kinds of information people are seeking
4. Market the library's information services in the community
5. Increase number of efficient public Internet workstations
6. Create visible "reference" or "information" kiosk staffed by a librarian who will answer questions
7. Provide consistent computer workstation support
8. Develop subject-specific workshops on finding information
9. Develop standardized research guides on popular topics
10. Survey library customers when leaving the library/library website as to whether they found information that met their needs

FIGURE 2.2

LIBRARY PLANNING CHECKLIST

To compete seriously for a grant, review your library's organizational attributes periodically by considering each of the following:

☐ Does your library have a clearly defined mission statement that is the foremost consideration in all decision making?

☐ Are your goals obtainable and supportive of your library's mission?

☐ Are your objectives clear, measurable, and tied to goal achievement?

☐ Do you periodically evaluate your objectives to be certain progress is being made?

☐ Have you selected a strategy for collecting data on your community and library?

☐ Are statistics aggregated to allow for easy retrieval of necessary information?

☐ Are you recording all participants' attendance in all of your programs and projects, their feedback after their participation, and the participants' demographics?

☐ Are all statistics that are collected actually used?

☐ Are you involving library staff and community members in the planning process?

☐ Did you communicate the final plan to staff, leadership, and community members?

☐ Do you have an accurate timetable for implementation of your library's plan, and have you designated specific dates for assessing progress toward goals?

☐ Are the library's programs, services, and projects current?

☐ Have you reviewed the latest needs among the population or community that your library serves?

☐ Are all programs, services, and operations conducted in a lean but sustainable fashion?

☐ Are all unnecessary expenses cut, savings implemented, and fundraising for each program and project stepped up?

☐ Are you reporting all bookkeeping and accounting thoroughly and honestly, and does your library complete grant reports and donor requests on time and honestly?

☐ Does your library use public relations and marketing opportunities to share successes and achievements and to thank the community for its support, or does the community only hear about budget cuts and closings?

☐ Are your leadership, beneficiaries, staff, and volunteers sharing information about their work with the library, and why they've chosen to become involved with it, with their friends, colleagues, and family?

Discovering and Designing the Grant Project

In chapter 2, we discussed the planning process that you, other library staff, community members, partners, and stakeholders participated in to assess and analyze the needs of your community and your organization in order to devise a strategic plan to meet those needs. You looked at the gaps between what your library currently offers and the desired results, and you decided which gaps you want to address in the time period covered by your plan. Then you developed and defined goals as well as specific, measurable, achievable, realistic, and time-bound objectives and activities designed to close the gaps. In this chapter, we cover project discovery and design during which you will develop a goal, objectives, and activities for a project. You will continue the process by creating a budget, timeline, and evaluation plan to complete the project plan. Funders want to see that you have thought through in some detail how your project will work and how it will yield the desired results. This chapter shows you how. When you plan a project this way, you will be creating many elements that will become part of your grant proposal.

Before we describe the project planning process, it is important first to clarify and establish some important terms and concepts about what a grant project is, the teams involved in grant work, and the importance of partners and collaborators.

What Is a Grant Project?

In this book, "grant project" refers to a library project, program, or service of any kind for which you will be writing a proposal to seek grant funding from an outside source. Other resources might define "grant project" differently. Don't let this confuse you. At this point, we are concentrating on discovering and designing your potential grant projects—regardless of what kind they are.

A grant project can be an equipment project, a capital project, a planning or implementation project, a research project, a model demonstration project, or a project for operating expenses, to name a few. It can be a children's program, a program for adults or teens, or services to meet a need in the community. In chapter 4, we focus on the kinds of projects you have developed as

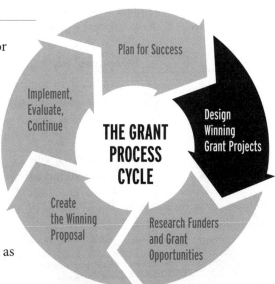

we look more closely at identifying specific funding sources and the types of projects they fund.

You will discover your grant project by beginning to work with the goals, objectives, and activities in your library's strategic plan. With your strategic plan in place, you have what you need to design grant projects that are directly related to the library's plan. Because they come straight from your strategic plan, these grant projects will inherently be mission driven and designed to meet specific identified needs in your community.

What Does Project Planning Have to Do with Winning Grants?

Discovering and designing your grant project and proposal writing are closely linked. Proposal writing does not stand alone or separately from project planning. As you define your project, you will be designing (and sometimes even writing) your proposal. By planning your project before sitting down to write your proposal, you are ensuring that your project comes from your desire to meet real needs in your community, you are working within the vision and mission of your organization, and your project is an integral part of your library's strategic plan. Proposals written from this perspective have a better success rate than those that are written without a clear plan. Funders want you to demonstrate that you have thought through your project, and they need assurance that you are capable of implementing it successfully.

Attempting to write your grant proposal before planning your project puts the primary focus on getting the dollars, not on implementing a project that meets your community's needs. If you approach proposal writing this way, you may end up with a grant that does not address the needs of your community or is not tied to your organization's mission or planned path. Project planning based on your library's strategic plan not only orients you within the existing plans and mission of your organization but also will keep you focused on working to better the lives of people in your community. Remember: grants are about the people, not the money.

It is essential that your projects emerge from your strategic plan, as this is the groundwork and the foundation you have built to serve your community and its specific needs. Ideally, you have already done this planning for your library, so all you need to do is pull out the plan and start working. If you have not done your strategic planning, consider stopping here and taking the time to do it. Going through the organizational planning process first will save you lots of time and headaches in the end and increase your chances of being funded. Planning first will ensure that you are developing projects that are in sync with your mission, projects that will benefit your community, and projects that include potential partners. Creating the plan first will decrease the chances that you will spend your valuable time on a project that has no real benefit to the community, does not include partners, and is not in line with your organizational goals. Planning first will increase your chances of winning grants.

Teams in Grant Work

Project planning is a team activity. Planning projects in isolation is very difficult. Planning takes a group of creative thinkers who represent library staff, the library board, the community, potential partners and collaborators, and other stakeholders. Team members bring creative ideas from different perspectives and increase your chances of success. Including potential partners and collaborators on your planning team allows you to utilize their specialized expertise and get their buy-in from the start.

Project planning teams could be a subset of the strategic planning team or an outgrowth of that team's work. They could consist of a new group of people convened around a particular set of library priorities, such as technology or digital resources. In larger organizations, departments or units responsible for a specific aspect of library service, such as the children's department in a public library or library instruction in a university library, usually lead the planning of projects in their areas of expertise. Your organization, its size, and the priorities from your strategic plan will determine the size and nature of your project planning teams.

In grant work there are different teams to plan projects, write proposals, and implement grant projects. As you have already learned, planning projects, writing proposals, and implementing projects are not solitary activities. This section explores the different kinds of teams, their roles, and their importance in your success with grants.

Project Planning Team

Project planning teams work to discover and design projects that arise directly from your strategic plan. They go through the project planning process described later in this chapter. Their work is done when they have produced plans for projects that are designed to help reach the library's goals and objectives. These teams consist of creative thinkers that include library staff, community members, potential partners, local businesspeople, and other stakeholders. They include people from potential partner organizations who you think may be participating in implementing a community project in which the library could be a partner. If you are in a large organization, you may want to create more than one project planning team, one for each organizational goal. These teams will include different people with different areas of expertise or community involvement depending on the goal with which they are working. If you are in a small library, a team of two people may be sufficient. Try to include one person from outside the library, preferably from another organization or agency in your community, a potential partner, or a prominent business leader. It is sometimes difficult to think creatively about new project ideas on a team consisting of all library staff who see one another daily and deal with the same issues continuously.

Proposal Writing Team (or Grant Team)

This team compiles and writes the grant proposal, secures all required signatures, checks for errors, and mails the proposal on time. Someone on this team is the contact person should the funder have questions or concerns. They follow up with the funder after submission and take responsibility for follow-up activities with the funder and the library when the proposal is successful.

Project Implementation Team

This team, consisting of library staff, consultants, partner staff, volunteers, and others, is responsible for making the project happen. They do the work of the activities, track their progress, measure their effectiveness, and make adjustments in the project activities as necessary. A project implementation team has a team leader, or project manager, to oversee all activities and act as the liaison with the library, the larger organization, staff, and funders. Some team members may have been part of the planning and proposal writing process; however, other team members may have been hired or selected only for the purpose of helping to implement this project.

Importance of Partners and Collaborators

It is very important to include potential partners from the very beginning in the project planning process. Ideas from potential partners are invaluable as you discover new projects. These people tend to look at things from a different angle, and they may even tell you about related activities they are already doing in the community of which you are unaware. This information can help to shape the project planning process and is likely to save you time and effort in the long run. By including potential partners from the community in project planning, you will decrease your chances of developing an idea that has already been planned or is already being done by another local organization or agency. In addition, partners can build on your ideas during the planning stages, bringing a dimension to your projects that you might never have considered without their perspective, knowledge, talents, and resources.

All communities have real needs that the library can help fulfill. The most urgent situations require a concerted team effort that will bring together the contributions of many talented individuals and responsible organizations. As has been said before, "None of us is as smart as all of us." By combining the resources of several entities, the library is better positioned to solve community problems. If your partners participate in the planning of library projects from the beginning, you will not have to go out into the community later to convince them to join you in supporting an idea that library staff have already planned. Also, if they are in on creating the project from the beginning, they will already have ownership without lots of extra effort on your part.

For a partnership to work, there must be common goals, mutual responsibilities, shared rewards, and plenty of communication. You will find that many organizations in your community share the same goals as your library, whether it be eradicating illiteracy, helping teens develop into accomplished individuals, or bridging the digital divide. Sharing the workload and the resources is of course a good thing, but good communication is essential. There should be a project director or someone designated to represent each partner. A partnership agreement or memorandum of understanding (MOU) can be used to specify the details of your partnership in writing. This can help avoid many common difficulties that collaborators often encounter. A Grant Partnership Agreement Worksheet that you can use in your library is included in part III (see p. 168) and online (www .alaeditions.org/webextras).

Many funders request or require that partners or collaborators be involved in your grant project. Funders across the board are looking for partnerships and collaborations among community organizations in grant applications. The basic reason for this is that they realize the greater the number of people at the table, the higher the probability of success and the bigger the impact of the funding. Funders know their dollars will go much further if more than one organization is involved in developing and implementing a project. They also know that a project is more likely to make a difference in the lives of people and more likely to be sustainable when more than one organization is committed to making it work.

Of course, it is impossible to predict who will be the ideal partners for your projects before you have even planned them. Use your best judgment based on what you know about your organization's strategic goals and objectives, projects already going on in your community, other organizations' activities in the community that might combine well with potential library projects, and business and organizational leaders who are likely to be good partners and with whom your library already has good relationships. If you discover during the project planning process that you have overlooked potential partners, invite them into the process right away.

The Project Planning Process

To recap, the preliminary steps in the project design process that we have covered so far include these:

1. Conducting a community needs assessment that identifies the areas that need change or improvement or the problems to be solved in the community
2. Strategic planning that outlines the solutions—or goals, objectives, and activities—that you have identified for the period covered by the plan
3. Seeking community input, the participation of stakeholders, and relationships with potential partners that have been established as a foundation for project planning and implementation
4. Forming a project planning team that includes library staff, community members, potential partners, local businesspeople, and other stakeholders

When you have a community needs assessment, a strategic plan with community involvement, and a project planning team in place, you are ready to plan library programs, services, and projects designed to meet community needs. The following steps will lead you through the process from beginning to end, starting with clarifying your library's goals, objectives, and activities in the strategic plan through to a well-developed project plan ready to adapt to a grant proposal or implement if you have sufficient funds. Your project plans will provide you with the basic components necessary for a grant application.

FIGURE 3.1		

SAMPLE STRATEGIC PLAN WORKSHEET: PREMIERE COMMUNITY LIBRARY 2016–2018

GOALS	OBJECTIVES	ACTIVITIES
Goal 1 The Premiere Community Library's resources and services are culturally sensitive, and they are designed to meet the diverse and changing information needs of the community.	**Objective 1.1** By July 2017, provide 50 percent more services and programs to meet the needs of Spanish-speaking community members.	1. Partner with local ESL teachers 2. Perform assessment of Spanish-speaking community members' needs 3. Collaborate with other local agencies serving the Spanish-speaking population 4. Provide staff training on cultural awareness, sensitivity, and service 5. Revise current library policies that impact delivery of services for Spanish speakers 6. Hire a bilingual librarian 7. Make website accessible for Spanish speakers 8. Market library to Spanish speakers in the community in their native language 9. Involve Spanish-speaking community members in planning
	Objective 1.2 By December 2016, provide at least three programs to serve the growing population of refugees from foreign nations.	1. Provide staff training on cultural awareness, sensitivity, and service 2. Investigate refugees' information needs 3. Involve native speakers as interpreters and library liaisons 4. Perform outreach to these new populations in neighborhoods and schools 5. Revise current library policies that impact delivery of services for this population 6. Provide programs to address their needs in neighborhood locations 7. Partner with other local agencies serving these populations 8. Make website accessible for these populations 9. Market library in their communities and in their languages 10. Involve refugee populations in planning
	Objective 1.3 By July 2018, increase by 50 percent the number of programs that bring together multiple diverse populations.	1. Using evaluations from programs for all segments of the population, plan programs to serve the entire community 2. Involve liaisons and representatives from diverse populations in planning 3. Market programs community-wide in multiple languages

GOALS	OBJECTIVES	ACTIVITIES
Goal 2 The Premiere Community Library serves the lifelong learning, informational, and leisure needs of the community's growing mature adult population.	**Objective 2.1** By the end of 2017, at least 40 percent of the adult population aged 55 and older will be registered library users.	1. Conduct a needs assessment to determine lifelong learning, informational, and leisure needs of the mature adult population 2. Assess all possible barriers in library and on the website for people aged 55 and older 3. Evaluate library's ADA (Americans with Disabilities) compliance 4. Conduct promotion with incentives to sign up people aged 55 and older 5. Perform outreach to older adults in assisted-living facilities and those who are homebound 6. Partner with local agencies that serve older adults 7. Spotlight materials in areas of the collection and on the website that are heavily used by older adults 8. Develop collections, provide programs, and offer services with people aged 55 and older in mind
	Objective 2.2 By the end of 2017, participation in programs geared toward mature adults will increase by 30 percent.	1. Organize speakers for seminars on health and wellness, retirement, financial and legal issues, relationships and stress in retirement, working in retirement, leisure and volunteer pursuits, Social Security and Medicare 2. Provide computer training that will help older adults find information they need 3. Spotlight library materials relating to programs for older adults 4. Create a page on the library's website with useful information and links for older adults 5. Make programs fun by including music, prizes, opportunities for communicating together, crafts, and so forth
Goal 3 The Premiere Community Library strives to educate the community about the information in the library, how to access it, and the importance of evaluating information prior to making important life decisions.	**Objective 3.1** During 2017, the library will increase programming that helps people use technology to access the information they need by 100 percent.	1. Find out what kinds of information people are seeking 2. Reallocate staff time to provide training and plan programming 3. Develop programs designed to meet people's specific information needs, such as Social Security, health information, applying to college, finding a job, homework help, and so forth 4. Provide training on how to find information using the library's website 5. Provide training on how to search the Internet effectively 6. Provide training on evaluating online information 7. Provide instruction on the use of online catalog and research databases
	Objective 3.2 By July 2018, 10 percent more community members who were not previous library users will indicate that the library met their information needs.	1. Perform outreach activities to nonlibrary users 2. Actively seek and respond to collection development suggestions from the community at large 3. Find out what kinds of information people are seeking 4. Market the library's information services in the community 5. Increase number of efficient public Internet workstations 6. Create visible "reference" or "information" kiosk staffed by a librarian who will answer questions 7. Provide consistent computer workstation support 8. Develop subject-specific workshops on finding information 9. Develop standardized research guides on popular topics 10. Survey library customers when leaving the library/library website as to whether they found information that met their needs

When project planning emerges from your library's strategic plan, your priority is meeting community needs. You are not preoccupied by chasing after a grant because you have not yet identified one. It is impossible to identify the right grant before you have planned a project. After your project design is in place, you will know what grants to seek that will help you implement the project. By planning the project first, you will already have the main components for your application in place by the time you identify the right grant.

Step 1: Clarify Your Library's Goals, Objectives, and Activities

Placing your library's goals, objectives, and activities into a chart will help you see them clearly (see figure 3.1). The chart will also serve as a starting point for the project planning team and quickly orient team members who may not be very familiar with the library's strategic plan.

It is always wise to have the strategic plan and/or a chart close at hand during project planning to serve as a compass to remind team members where the library is headed. Use the Strategic Plan Worksheet provided in part III (see p. 170) and online (www .alaeditions.org/webextras) to chart your organization's goals, objectives, and activities.

Step 2: Start the Project Planning Process

The project planning process must be facilitated. Someone needs to be responsible for leading the project planning team through the process of discovering and designing the project. This person could be a member of the library staff who was instrumental in the strategic planning process, or if you have the funds, you could hire an outside consultant to facilitate this process. In general, planning is easier, more efficient, and more effective when an objective third person is responsible for keeping things on track. It is very difficult to facilitate and participate at the same time; however, if you do not have enough staff or money for a separate facilitator, this can be done. Just be aware of the pitfalls and appoint someone who can play the two roles without confusing them. If you are a one- or two-person library, you can share the role of facilitating. In short, this process cannot be left to the free-flowing organic method and be expected to conclude with a viable project plan. Project planning is a focused and purposeful activity.

At the first meeting of your project planning team, it is important to orient team members to their purpose and to answer their questions. Distribute copies of your library's Strategic Plan Goals, Objectives, and Activities Chart to all project planning team members. (This is the Strategic Plan Worksheet from part III that you completed in step 1.) The team's first task is to understand the library's vision, mission, service responses to the community, goals, objectives, and activities. It may be necessary to share some background information about the community needs assessment and how the goals were determined for those team members who were not involved in the strategic planning process.

If you have convened the team to design a specific project to address a particular need, such as an improved literacy rate, let them know this focus from the start. Make it clear to the team members that their purpose is to plan a project to address certain goals, objectives, and activities in the library's plan. Explain that the library will be working over the next few years on multiple projects designed to accomplish different goals established in the plan. The team is not expected to tackle all the elements in your plan by thinking up projects to accomplish all the goals in the library's plan.

Step 3: Discover the Project Idea and Goals

Encourage brainstorming and creativity, but keep the parameters of the projects you are planning within the scope of the library's strategic plan. Keep team members focused on the particular need they are addressing without restricting their thinking about project design. You may want to come up with one or several smaller projects to start. As you work with the smaller projects, you can try combining several of them into one larger project. It is much easier to grow a project than to shrink it. Also, your project can accomplish more and make a bigger difference in people's lives when you combine several smaller ideas. But be careful not to overreach the library's capabilities. Be realistic.

Make this a fun activity for the whole team. Use flip charts, colored index cards, markers, scissors, favors or prizes for the best ideas, or group activities, for example. Move around. Brainstorm. Try dividing the larger group into smaller groups of three or four people. If the team is working on designing projects for multiple goals, you could assign each group a goal and then tell group members that they can draw from any related objective or activity to accomplish the goal. Give them permission to expand or alter the objectives and to create new activities for the purposes of this process, as long as they still address reaching the goals and objectives stated in the plan. Try to remove any barriers that you think may be restricting this process without compromising the library's strategic plan. Remember to record all ideas and compile them into one document for team members to use in future meetings as they work through project ideas. Have fun!

Avoid talking about money or how the project will be funded at this stage. It is likely to come up, so be prepared. Some librarians are well practiced at saying there is not enough money to implement creative projects. This is one way to quickly stop creative ideas in their tracks. It will prevent any chance of designing innovative projects to meet community needs. If any projects the team designs require supplemental funding, they may become grant projects. The purpose of this book is to show you how to fund projects you cannot fund with your current budget.

The following is an example project idea developed from the Premiere Community Library's strategic plan.

Information at Your Fingertips Project Idea

The Premiere Community Library in partnership with the Premiere Community College and the Premiere Diversity Center will focus on educating adults in the diverse community about information they can find online, how to evaluate it, and how to use it. This project will assess unmet information needs of diverse communities such as Spanish-speaking community members and the growing refugee population; reach out to nonlibrary users; and provide training on how to find information and search databases, effectively search for information online, and evaluate information.

Developing the Sample Project Idea

Next, the Information at Your Fingertips project idea needs goals, objectives, and activities. Every project must have a goal. The goal is the result you seek. Ask what you are seeking to accomplish. How do you want your services, situation, or community to change as a result of your efforts? It is important not to confuse goals with organizational mission or vision. The goal must be consistent with your mission and vision but also program specific.

Any or all of the goals in the Premiere Community Library's strategic plan could be used to develop a goal for the Information at Your Fingertips project. By addressing the target populations—people whose first language is not English and the growing refugee population—within your library's existing goals, you can easily develop potential project goals. Your project can incorporate any or all of the goals from your library plan, and you can also develop other project goals as long as they are within the framework of your library's plan. At this point, it is worthwhile to develop some "working" project goals so you can stay focused on developing and designing a manageable project. You can always come back to these goals and rework them, if necessary, or replace them with new ones you missed the first time around.

For the purposes of illustrating the process, let's choose some working project goals, for instance:

- Diverse community members will easily find and evaluate information they need using the library's resources and databases and other online resources.
- The library is responsive to the changing information needs of diverse populations in our community.
- The library successfully serves diverse communities in the library and on the library's website.

Step 4: Define the Project Outcomes

The Importance of Outcomes

As you begin to discover your project ideas, it is important to think about outcomes. Outcomes are used to identify a change in behavior, attitude, skill, life condition, or knowledge in the people served by the project, and they reflect the long-term impact a project will make toward solving a community problem or improving the lives of the people it serves. Most funders require applicants to state the outcomes of their project in the proposal. The time to establish the outcomes is when you are planning the project. That a library proposes to provide assistive technology, Spanish-language materials, after-school programs, information technology training, 3-D printers, or any other service is admirable, but the funder wants to know that those services will make a difference in the lives of the people who are served and also how they will make a difference. You want to make sure that the project will address or solve a problem in the community by changing the behavior, attitude, or knowledge of the people served by the project, but you also need to know how your project will accomplish these things and to what degree. This is not only good practice; it also makes good sense whether you will be funding the project with a grant or not.

From the preliminary project planning stage and throughout the planning process, continue to ask yourself these questions:

1. How will the project help to solve a problem or meet a need in the community?
2. How will the project improve the lives of the people we serve?
3. How will people's behavior, attitude, or knowledge change as a result of the project?

Asking these questions of yourself periodically will help you to focus on why this project is needed in your community. Staying grounded in the difference it will make for your community is essential. It is not uncommon for personal wants and desires to sneak in during the planning process, and checking in with these questions is a good way to keep all team members together on the right track.

If you do not clarify your project outcomes from the outset, it will be much more difficult to build them in later when you are preparing your grant proposal. So, let's develop some desired outcomes for the Information at Your Fingertips project. Remember, outcomes identify a change in behavior, attitude, or knowledge in the people served by the project. As we think about outcomes for this project, we might want to focus on a particular subject or topic of interest to Spanish-speaking community members and the growing refugee population. We might want to address a specific segment of information technology or work on the usability of the library's website for people whose first language is not English. Some desired outcomes for this project idea might be as follows:

1. Knowing how to use the library or library's website to find information will increase the ability of Spanish-speaking community members and people from foreign countries to make informed choices.
2. Community members who are from foreign countries and/or whose first language is not English will know about the information technology available in the library, and they will know how to use it to improve their quality of life.
3. As a result of library programs and seminars designed to meet their needs, Spanish-speaking community members and newly arrived refugees will gain knowledge that will help improve their life condition.

More about the Definitions of Outcomes and Objectives

Outcomes and objectives present a unique challenge. Funders do not always use the same definitions when it comes to outcomes and objectives. The definitions for goals, outcomes, objectives, and activities or action steps can vary widely by funder. What one funder considers an outcome, another may consider an objective. In some cases, your goal may actually be an outcome. Remember that you are trying to identify a

FIGURE 3.2

SAMPLE PROJECT PLANNING WORKSHEET: INFORMATION AT YOUR FINGERTIPS PROJECT

1. Project Description
Briefly describe your project. Include why you are doing this project, who will benefit, what you will do, where it will take place, and with whom.

The Premiere Community Library in partnership with the Premiere Community College and the Premiere Diversity Center will focus on educating adults in the diverse community about information they can find online, how to evaluate it, and how to use it. This project will assess unmet information needs of diverse communities such as Spanish-speaking community members and the growing refugee population; reach out to nonlibrary users; and provide training on how to find information and search databases, effectively search for information online, and evaluate information.

2. Keywords
List keywords that describe your project.

Adults	Community
Diversity	Library
Spanish speakers	Public awareness
Information technology	Refugees
Computers	Classes
Website	Training
Online information	Information evaluation

3. Needs Statement
Describe the need in your community or the problem your project will address.

Lack of awareness of library's services and resources among the diverse community including Spanish speakers and the growing refugee population; lack of knowledge among this population about how to search for information online and evaluate it; lack of training in their native language about finding information, searching databases, and evaluating information online

4. Target Audience
Describe the target audience for the project.

Adults in the community who are Spanish speakers and members of the growing refugee population

5. Project Goals
List the goals of the project.

1. Diverse community members will easily find and evaluate information they need using the library's resources and databases and other online resources.
2. The library is responsive to the changing information needs of diverse populations in our community.
3. The library successfully serves diverse communities in the library and on the library's website.

6. Project Outcomes
Describe how the project will impact a community problem and list the outcomes for people in terms of what knowledge they will gain, what skills they will learn, which behaviors will change, how their quality of life will improve, and so forth.

1. Knowing how to use the library or library's website to find information will increase the ability of Spanish-speaking community members and people from foreign countries to make informed choices.
2. Community members who are from foreign countries and/or whose first language is not English will know about the information technology available in the library, and they will know how to use it to improve their quality of life.
3. As a result of library programs and seminars designed to meet their needs, Spanish-speaking community members and newly arrived refugees will gain knowledge that will help improve their life condition.

7. Project Objectives

List SMART (specific, measurable, achievable, realistic, and time-bound) objectives for the project. Explain how you will know when you have solved this problem.

1. By July 2018, there will be 25 percent more registered library cardholders in the three area codes with the greatest number of people who are Spanish speakers and members of the growing refugee population.
2. By September 2018, 50 percent of the people in the target population who attend classes about how to find information online will say their knowledge increased.
3. By December 2018, 75 percent of the target population who use the library's website will say they had the ability to find the information they needed.
4. By December 2018, 25 percent of people in the community who speak Spanish or who are members of the growing refugee population will know how to find information in the library and online and how to evaluate it.

8. Project Action Steps

List the steps or activities required to make the changes listed above. Develop strategies and a timeline required to reach the objectives.

See Sample Project Action Steps (figure 3.3).
See Sample Project Timeline (figure 3.4).

9. Resources Needed

List the resources you will need to accomplish the steps. Note the resources you already have.

Computer lab	Telephones
Meeting rooms	Copier
Office supplies	Projector
Staff	

10. Partners and Collaborators

List your partners on this project. Note who else is likely to help you address this problem in your community.

Premiere Diversity Center
Literacy Center of Premiere
Premiere Community College

11. Project Budget

Detail how much this project will cost to implement.

See Sample Project Budgets (figures 3.5, 3.6, and 3.7).

12. Evaluation

Describe how you will measure your success to show that you have reached your objectives.

See Sample Evaluation Plan (figure 3.8).

desired change and to measure that change, regardless of what the funder calls it. Proposal writers who fail to recognize the differences in how funders define terms may be unsuccessful because they present their information incorrectly.

While the definitions of goals, outcomes, and objectives may vary by funder, you can manage these differences by investigating a little further. If a funder uses an example, follow it back to your own goals, outcomes, and objectives. Use the funder's language and definitions for the purposes of submitting your proposal. If you have done all the work to this point, it is fairly simple to label proposal elements differently to comply with the funder's guidelines. The basic elements of your plan will not change. If you are not sure about a funder's definitions, contact the funder and ask.

Step 5: Plan Your Project

Now it's time to plan your project. Start using the Project Planning Worksheet provided in part III (see p. 174) and online (www.alaeditions.org/webextras) to help you develop your own project ideas. Based on the planning we have done so far, try working on #1–#7: Project Description, Keywords, Needs Statement, Target Audience, Project Goals, Project Outcomes, and Project Objectives. Make sure that these elements tie in to your library's plan, vision, and mission. Don't spend too much time on perfecting the worksheet at this point. It is meant to facilitate the project design process, help you work out some of the details, record your ideas, and test their feasibility. Think of it as a project outline tool. Use a new Project Planning Worksheet for each new project idea. Figure 3.2 provides an example Project Planning Worksheet for the Information at Your Fingertips project that you can use as a guide as you do this work in your library.

Step 6: Develop Project Objectives

You must design specific, measurable, achievable, realistic, and time-bound objectives that specifically address your project outcomes. You may find that you can use objectives already developed in your strategic plan; however, it is more likely that your project objectives will be a subset or adaptation of the objectives in your library's plan.

Going back to the library's strategic plan and your working project goals and established outcomes, ask yourself how you will demonstrate that the Information at Your Fingertips project was a success. For instance, how will you show that as a result (or outcome) of the project more Spanish-speaking community members and members of the growing refugee population will be able to find something that meets their information needs during a visit to the library or the library's website? Some possible objectives that could demonstrate this outcome include these:

1. By July 2018, there will be 25 percent more registered library cardholders in the three area codes with the greatest number of people who are Spanish speakers and members of the growing refugee population.
2. By September 2018, 50 percent of the people in the target population who attend classes about how to find information online will say their knowledge increased.

3. By December 2018, 75 percent of the target population who use the library's website will say they had the ability to find the information they needed.
4. By December 2018, 25 percent of people in the community who speak Spanish or who are members of the growing refugee population will know how to find information in the library and online and how to evaluate it.
5. By July 2018, 20 percent more Spanish-speaking community members and members of the growing refugee population will know about the information they can find during a visit to the library or the library's website.

Review the objectives for your project as listed in your Project Planning Worksheet and make adjustments as necessary. Remember to keep the objectives specific, measurable, achievable, realistic, and time-bound. It is important to have these objectives in place from the beginning because eventually you will use them to design your evaluation methodology.

Step 7: Define Project Action Steps

Next it is time to develop the action steps that will accomplish your project's objectives and produce the desired outcomes. Review the working project goals and sample project objectives and outcomes in the Project Planning Worksheet for the Information at Your Fingertips project. What action steps might help achieve the sample project goals, objectives, and outcomes? Here are several examples:

- Conduct a needs assessment and ongoing focus groups with Spanish-speaking community members and members of the growing refugee population to determine their current and changing information needs.
- Hire library liaisons to work with Spanish-speaking community members and members of the growing refugee population.
- Recruit Spanish-speaking community members and members of the growing refugee population as library customers.
- Reduce language barriers in the library and on the library's website for Spanish-speaking community members and members of the growing refugee population.
- Spotlight library materials in areas heavily used by Spanish-speaking community members and members of the growing refugee population.
- Develop a collection development plan that is responsive to current topics of interest to Spanish-speaking community members and members of the growing refugee population and that accommodates their needs.
- Organize speakers, workshops, and programs for Spanish-speaking community members and members of the growing refugee population on topics of interest to them and that are important to their quality of life.
- Develop a curriculum and implement classes to teach Spanish-speaking community members and members of the growing refugee population about how to use information technology to find what they need in the library and on the library's website.

- Develop standardized research guides on topics of interest to Spanish-speaking community members and members of the growing refugee population.
- Cooperate actively with other community agencies serving Spanish-speaking community members and members of the growing refugee population to share resources and provide services.
- Conduct pre- and post-tests, administer surveys, and use other evaluation methods to measure the progress of the project.

FIGURE 3.3

SAMPLE PROJECT ACTION STEPS: INFORMATION AT YOUR FINGERTIPS PROJECT

OBJECTIVES	PERSONNEL	ACTION STEPS
By July 2018, there will be 25 percent more registered library cardholders in the three area codes with the greatest number of people who are Spanish speakers and members of the growing refugee population.	Circulation Librarian	• Determine three area codes with the greatest number of Spanish speakers and refugees. • Generate and analyze cardholder data in the three area codes. • Create baseline and target numbers.
	Library Assistant	• Track statistics. • Assist with library card sign-up campaigns.
	Outreach Librarian	• Determine locations and methods for outreach in three area codes. • Work with community agencies to reach target population. • Organize, schedule, and coordinate library card sign-up campaigns. • Hold public awareness activities. • Engage with the community.
	Marketing Librarian	• Create brochures, flyers, and website banners to advertise.
By September 2018, 50 percent of the people in the target population who attend classes about how to find information online will say their knowledge increased.	Instruction Librarian	• Design classes to teach diverse community members how to find information. • Teach classes. • Conduct pre- and post-tests/surveys. • Incorporate web features.
	Outreach Librarian	• Conduct a needs assessment. • Engage with the community. • Recruit participants. • Conduct focus groups and interviews.
	Library Assistant	• Advertise classes. • Schedule classes. • Reserve computer classroom. • Register participants. • Track computer usage. • Track statistics.
	Marketing Librarian	• Create brochures, flyers, and website banners to advertise.

Note that these action steps are either taken directly from activities in the Premiere Community Library's Strategic Plan Worksheet (see figure 3.1), adapted from activities in the plan, or enhance activities already in the plan.

What are some action steps that might help you accomplish your project goal through your stated objectives and result in the outcomes you have identified? Use the Project Action Steps Worksheet provided in part III (see p. 176) and online (www.alaeditions .org/webextras) to define your project's action steps. Figure 3.3 shows an example of

OBJECTIVES	PERSONNEL	ACTION STEPS
By December 2018, 75 percent of the target population who use the library's website will say they had the ability to find the information they needed.	Webmaster	• Assess website usability for Spanish-speaking people and refugee population. • Make changes to accommodate target population.
	Outreach Librarian	• Conduct needs assessment. • Conduct pre- and post-surveys. • Make website recommendations.
	Technology Librarian	• Troubleshoot website issues reported by the target population.
	Reference Librarian	• Assist people with finding the information they need. • Track questions. • Make recommendations to Technology Librarian and Webmaster.
By December 2018, 25 percent of people who speak Spanish or who are members of the growing refugee population will know how to find information in the library and online and how to evaluate it.	Outreach Librarian	• Conduct a needs assessment. • Engage with the community. • Recruit participants. • Conduct focus groups and interviews.
	Library Assistant	• Advertise classes. • Schedule classes. • Reserve computer classroom. • Register participants. • Track computer usage. • Track statistics.
	Instruction Librarian	• Conduct pre- and post-surveys. • Develop a class on library resources and how to evaluate information. • Teach classes. • Develop an online tutorial. • Create a video. • Teach classes.

the action steps for the Information at Your Fingertips project, including the personnel who will do the activities and the objectives that the action steps will address. As you complete this worksheet for your project, think about who will be doing the action steps and enter the position name in the Personnel column. Feel free to come up with new ideas that are specific to your project. It's okay to brainstorm here; however, make sure any new ideas relate back to the goals and objectives in your strategic plan. In your grant proposal, the action steps and who will do them will become your methodology, strategy, or approach. This information eventually becomes the basis for your timeline.

Step 8: Do the Research

As you are planning your project, read about other projects like yours that have already been done. Take notes and collect this research. Based on the experiences or products of others, you may want to alter your project. It makes sense to build on what others have done. If there are curricula already in place that will meet your project's needs, use them. If another community like yours had success reaching a similar target population, learn from their successes—and failures. Build this experience and research into your project plan. It will be more viable, be more likely to succeed, and have a better chance of being sustainable. Call or e-mail the manager of a project like the one you are considering and ask him or her to share experiences. Conversely, know the pitfalls of projects like yours and build in preventative measures. Note the resources you will need in #9 on your Project Planning Worksheet. Continue to add resources as you discover what you will need.

Include this information in your grant proposal. It shows the funder that you are well informed about what has already been done in the field and that you are knowledgeable about best practices. Extrapolate your outcomes to the outcomes documented in the literature. For instance, "Based on the results of XYZ Library, we have chosen to take ABC approach in our community." The funder wants to know that you will not be doing something that has already been tried without success. Let the funder know that you have educated yourself and you are in familiar territory.

As part of your research, investigate other agencies or organizations in your community that are doing similar work or serving the target population for your project. Record any potential partners in #10 on your Project Planning Worksheet.

Step 9: Make a Project Timeline

Timelines are project-planning tools that are used to represent the timing of tasks required to complete a project. They are easy to understand and construct, and most project managers use them to track the progress of a project. There are many ways to construct timelines. For our purposes, each action step takes up one row in a simple table. Dates run along the top row, with heading columns representing days, weeks, or months, depending on the total length of the project. Check marks or horizontal bars marking the expected beginning and end of the task represent the expected time for each task. Tasks may run sequentially, at the same time, or overlap each other. Include the personnel responsible for each action step. Use the Project Timeline Worksheet

FIGURE 3.4

SAMPLE PROJECT TIMELINE: INFORMATION AT YOUR FINGERTIPS PROJECT

ACTION STEPS	PERSONNEL	JAN	FEB	MAR	APR	MAY	JUNE	JULY	AUG	SEPT	OCT	NOV	DEC
Conduct needs assessments/focus groups	Outreach Librarian (OL)	●	●										
Determine location with most people in target population/Generate data	OL	●	●										
Hold public awareness campaigns/Register new users	OL					●	●						
Engage with community	OL	●		●	●	●	●	●	●	●	●	●	●
Create brochures/advertisements	Marketing Librarian (ML)		●	●	●	●	●						
Track statistics/computer usage	Library Assistant (LA)	●	●	●	●	●	●	●	●	●	●	●	●
Develop curricula	Instruction Librarian (IL)			●	●	●	●	●	●	●	●	●	
Design pre- and post-surveys/tests	IL			●	●	●	●			●			
Schedule classes/Reserve classroom	LA				●				●				
Advertise classes	LA			●	●	●	●	●	●	●	●	●	●
Register people for classes	LA				●	●	●	●	●	●	●	●	●
Teach classes	IL					●	●	●	●	●	●	●	
Create video	IL						●	●					
Develop online tutorial	IL								●	●			
Assess website usability	Webmaster (W)	●											
Make website accommodations	W		●	●	●								
Troubleshoot/monitor website issues for target population	Technology Librarian (TL)			●	●	●	●	●	●	●	●	●	●
Assist target population with finding information they need	Reference Librarian (RL)	●		●	●	●	●	●	●	●	●	●	●
Update website	W	●	●										
Project management	Library Director	●	●	●	●	●	●	●	●	●	●	●	●

provided in part III (see p. 177) and online (www.alaeditions.org/webextras) to create a timeline for your project.

In constructing a timeline, keep the tasks to a manageable number (no more than fifteen or twenty) so that the chart fits on a single page. If your project is complex, it may require subcharts and subtasks. This timeline can go directly into your grant proposal for this project. Figure 3.4 illustrates a timeline using the action steps we developed for the Information at Your Fingertips project.

Step 10: Develop a Project Budget

It is usually easier to develop a personnel budget and a nonpersonnel budget separately and then combine them at the end to total your project costs. Personnel budgets usually involve adding benefits, including salary projections, and adjusting FTEs (full-time equivalents), whereas nonpersonnel budgets are more straightforward, requiring less mathematical acrobatics. If you are working in a spreadsheet program such as Excel, it is usually simpler to keep these very different kinds of budgets separate as you are working on them. Additionally, presenting your budget in a way so that funders can clearly distinguish between personnel costs and nonpersonnel costs makes your proposal easier to read and interpret. You want to make reviewing your proposal a pleasant experience for funders.

Personnel Budget

Using your Project Timeline and Action Steps Worksheets, figure out the personnel and FTEs required for your project in the following way. First, select one position and determine the activities that position will do. For instance, for the Information at Your Fingertips project, the library assistant will perform these tasks:

- Prepare handouts and research guides
- Schedule speakers, workshops, and programs
- Implement pre- and post-surveys
- Calculate survey results
- Record focus groups
- Register people for classes

Next, determine the amount of time the position will be spending on these activities over the duration of the project and calculate the cost of the salary to cover that amount of time. For example, the library assistant will be doing the listed activities throughout the entire twelve-month period of the project, and we can estimate that this will take the library assistant an average of eight hours a week. Since the library assistant works forty hours a week, this is one-fifth, or .20 FTE, of the library assistant's time. The library assistant's full-time salary is $30,000 per year; therefore, the cost to the project for the library assistant's salary is $6,000.

Finally, calculate the cost of benefits for your project personnel, and make sure to add that cost to the project budget. Your personnel department will be able to tell you this figure or percentage. For example, if the cost of benefits to the organization is 23 percent of the employee's salary, for .20 ($6,000) of the library assistant's salary, that is $1,380. Therefore, the total cost to the project for the .20 FTE library assistant for the twelve-month duration of the project is $6,000 (salary) + $1,380 (benefits) = $7,380.

Go through the same process for all project personnel. Then create a personnel budget for your project using the Personnel Budget Worksheet provided in part III (see p. 178) and online (www.alaeditions.org/webextras). Don't forget to include fringe benefit costs for all personnel, and make sure to include or designate a project manager. Figure 3.5 shows a personnel budget for the Information at Your Fingertips project.

Cautionary note: If library staff will be working as project personnel, you must decrease their current job duties and responsibilities to allow for the additional project duties they will be taking on before they begin working on the funded project. For instance, if the previous library assistant currently works a forty-hour week, he already has job duties that take forty hours a week to do.

You must take away some of the regular job duties (by delegating to other staff or hiring another staff person) so project personnel can add the additional project duties. You cannot simply pile more work on a person who is already working a full-time job. This can be a setup for failure (for the project and for the staff member) and will ensure that a staff person will not want to participate in any more library grant projects in the future. Expecting staff to assume additional work because a project is funded is a common pitfall that must be avoided. This practice also sends a message to the larger organization that you will pile more work on your staff without compensating them. When things get tough economically, they will remember the library as a place to save money by reducing staff because the remaining staff will be happy to do more work without being compensated.

FIGURE 3.5

SAMPLE PERSONNEL BUDGET: INFORMATION AT YOUR FINGERTIPS PROJECT

POSITION	SALARY	BENEFITS (30%)	TOTAL
.05 FTE Library Director	$3,500	$1,050	$4,550
.50 FTE Outreach Librarian	27,000	8,100	35,100
.60 FTE Instruction Librarian	32,400	9,720	42,120
.20 FTE Library Assistant	5,000	1,500	6,500
.10 FTE Reference Librarian	5,500	1,650	7,150
.25 FTE Technology Librarian	13,500	4,050	17,550
.10 FTE Marketing Librarian	5,000	1,500	6,500
.05 FTE Webmaster	1,500	450	1,950
Total Personnel Costs	**$93,400**	**$28,020**	**$121,420**

Nonpersonnel Budget

Next, determine the cost for items other than personnel, such as marketing, equipment, space rental, and supplies. Develop a nonpersonnel budget for your project using the Nonpersonnel Budget Worksheet provided in part III (see p. 179) and online (www .alaeditions.org/webextras). See figure 3.6 for a sample nonpersonnel budget for the Information at Your Fingertips project.

Now create your project budget by combining the personnel budget and the nonpersonnel budget. Add the total costs from each to determine the total project cost and record this information on the Project Budget Worksheet provided in part III (see p. 180) and online (www.alaeditions.org/webextras). Record the total cost of your project in #11 on your Project Planning Worksheet.

Incorporating Match and In-Kind Funding into the Budget

When your library, your partners, or other grants have already committed funds, personnel, equipment, space, or other items to support a project, it is important to include this information in your project budget. This serves several purposes: (1) you can easily see what parts of your project have already been funded and what parts have not yet been funded; (2) it will be easier to spot a funding opportunity when you know the amount you need and exactly what it will fund; and (3) you can pitch your project idea in the community, focusing on the portion you still need to fund. If you have multiple sources of funding like this, it will be helpful to create a "working" budget that incorporates them all (see the example in figure 3.7). Eventually, when you submit a budget with your proposal, it will need to show all the sources of funding for your project.

Step 11: Create an Evaluation Plan

You must now determine how you will measure the effectiveness of your project in reaching your stated objectives and outcomes. How will you measure your progress? How will you measure your successes? How will you measure a change in behavior? How will you decide what adjustments need to be made to facilitate the success of your project as it progresses? It is important to understand why you must conduct an evaluation and why an evaluation plan is a necessary part of your project plan.

Projects are undertaken to have an impact. Evaluations are conducted to show the success of a project's impact, and they can also point out improvements you can make in the project design.

Evaluation Types

- *Formative*: Some funders prefer that you conduct evaluations throughout the life of the project rather than (or in addition to) evaluating the project at its end. These are called formative evaluations. The theory is that ongoing evaluations will enable project staff to measure the success of the project while

FIGURE 3.6

SAMPLE NONPERSONNEL BUDGET: INFORMATION AT YOUR FINGERTIPS PROJECT

ITEM	DESCRIPTION	COST
Marketing		
5,000 Brochures	1,000 for $800	$4,000
5,000 Flyers	@ $.20 each	1,000
5 Newspaper ads	$200 for quarter page	1,000
Equipment		
Projector		3,000
Copying Costs		
Class handouts, research guides	5,000 @ $.20/copy	1,000
Supplies		
Office supplies	$75/month ÷ 12	900
Printer cartridges	50 @ $70 each	3,500
Paper	100 reams @ $5/ream	500
Space Rental		
Computer classroom	600 sq.' @ $200/month ÷ 12	2,400
Travel		
Round trip for community outreach	10 trips @ $13/trip	130
Total Non-Personnel Costs		**$17,430**
Total Personnel Costs		**$121,420**
Total Project Cost		**$138,850**

it is being carried out and make needed adjustments throughout the life of the project to ensure its overall success.

- *Summative*: Some funders ask for one evaluation at the very end of the project that reports all accomplishments. This is known as a summative evaluation and stresses the outcome of the project.
- *Quantitative*: A quantitative evaluation answers the question, "How much did you do?" For examples: How many people attended a class? What skills did students learn? What was the cost to the project per student? Quantitative evaluations require obtaining and analyzing data over a large number of cases. Methods for collecting quantitative data include pre-tests and post-tests, questionnaires, and surveys.

FIGURE 3.7

SAMPLE WORKING BUDGET: INFORMATION AT YOUR FINGERTIPS PROJECT

PERSONNEL BUDGET

Position	Total Cost	Match	$ Requested
.05 FTE Library Director	$4,550	$4,550	
.50 FTE Outreach Librarian	35,100	15,100	$20,000
.60 FTE Instruction Librarian	42,120	12,120	$30,000
.20 FTE Library Assistant	6,500	6500	
.10 FTE Reference Librarian	7,150	2,150	5,000
.25 FTE Technology Librarian	17,550	7,550	10,000
.10 FTE Marketing Librarian	6,500	1,500	5,000
.05 FTE Webmaster	1,950	1,950	
Total personnel costs	**$121,420**	**$51,420**	**$70,000**

NONPERSONNEL BUDGET

Item	Total Cost	Match	$ Requested
Marketing	$6,000		$6,000
Equipment	3,000		$3,000
Copying Costs	1,000	1,000	
Supplies	4,900	2,000	2,900
Space Rental	2,400		2,400
Travel	130		130
Total Non-Personnel Costs	**$17,430**	**$3,000**	**$14,430**
Total Project Costs	**$138,850**	**$54,420**	**$84,430**

- *Qualitative*: Qualitative evaluations tell the project's story by communicating the participants' stories. They collect and examine data in greater depth on a smaller scale. Qualitative methods include interviews, case studies, observation, and documentation reviews telling what happened when, to whom, and with what consequences.

Your funder may require you to conduct only a summative evaluation at the end of the project. Don't limit your evaluation to the type required by the funder. Decide on an evaluation approach that serves the needs of your customers and that will best measure the success of your particular project. For some projects, you might want to conduct formative and summative evaluations or qualitative and quantitative evaluations.

Outcome-Based Evaluation

Outcome-based evaluation (OBE), an evaluation methodology that many government agencies and larger organizations have adopted for their programs, focuses on measuring the effect of a project on the people it serves (outcomes) rather than on the services (outputs). Outcome-based evaluation methods can be used at many points in a project to provide indicators of a project's effectiveness, and they provide a greater degree of public accountability. Critical feedback is given about what is working, what needs to be changed, and how a program can be improved.

Outcome-based evaluation measures results, making observations that demonstrate change, and systematically collects information about specific indicators to show the extent to which a project achieves its goals. As you may recall, an outcome is a measure of change that benefits the people served by your project, such as achievements or changes in skill, knowledge, attitude, behavior, condition, or life status. Examples of outcomes include the following:

- Library customers will know about the electronic resources available in the library. (Change in knowledge)
- Teen library users will view the library as a place to gather for studying and attend events with their friends. (Change in attitude)
- Assistive technology will enable people with disabilities to use library resources to improve their quality of life. (Change in condition)
- Mature adult customers will use library computers to stay in touch with family and friends. (Change in behavior)
- The ability of the unemployed to find jobs will be increased due to job-finding resources in the library. (Change in life status)

Methods for Collecting Evaluation Information and Data

Your objectives themselves will determine the types of information you need to collect. For instance, if an objective states that 20 percent more Spanish-speaking community members will find information that meets their needs during a visit to the library or the library's website, you will have to ask Spanish-speaking community members if they found the information they needed as they leave the library or website. In this case, a survey or questionnaire is the most appropriate tool for collecting this information.

There are many ways to collect evaluation information and data. Evaluation instruments can include questionnaires and surveys, interviews, documentation review, observation, focus groups, or case studies. It is important to use the proper evaluation instrument to measure your results. Decide which measurement instrument is most appropriate to get the strongest data specific to your project objectives.

QUESTIONNAIRES OR SURVEYS

You can get much information quickly and easily from many people in a nonthreatening way using questionnaires and surveys. People can complete them anonymously, they are inexpensive to administer, and you can administer them to many people. It is easy for you to compare and analyze results, and you can get lots of data. Information gathered from surveys is only as good as the questions you ask, so you might want to consult an experienced surveyor as you design the questions. There are many survey and questionnaire instruments that have already been designed that you can use as templates; however, make sure to customize them to your project. The shorter a survey is, the easier it will be for a busy customer to complete. Be sure to provide confidentiality to your survey participants. Reassuring your participants that their survey responses will be kept confidential and anonymous might help improve your response rates. Usually, asking participants to reveal their personal information like name, address, and phone number on a survey will reduce response rates.

There are online survey tools, such as SurveyMonkey and Google Forms, that you can use to survey people online. Remember that this approach will reach only those people who are online or who visit the library's website.

INTERVIEWS

Use interviews when you want to fully understand someone's impressions or experiences or to learn more about their answers in surveys or questionnaires. Interviews give you the opportunity to get the full range and depth of information and allow you to develop a rapport with the interviewee, and you can be flexible with your questioning. This method provides subjective data because it is based on opinions that may not reflect the true success of the project. It is a very time-consuming process, but it may yield future partners and project ideas. Interviews can add valuable information for outcome-based assessments because they may reveal changes in a person's behavior, attitude, skill, life condition, or knowledge.

DOCUMENTATION REVIEW

Use documentation reviews when you want an impression of how your project is operating without interrupting the project. This method is comprised of reviewing project statistics, memos, minutes, and so forth. Because this method does not measure changes in people's behaviors, skills, knowledge, attitudes, condition, or life status, use it only as a supplement to instruments that do measure these things.

OBSERVATION

By observing a project, you can gather accurate information about how it actually operates, particularly about the process. You view the operations of a project as they are actually occurring.

FOCUS GROUPS

Focus groups allow you to explore a topic in depth through group discussion, and they can provide very honest and useful information. You can get reactions to an experience or suggestion, and you can gain an understanding of common complaints. Focus group membership can be organized into manageable numbers. If the participants are comfortable, they may give very helpful feedback. This is an efficient way to get key information about a project, and you can quickly and reliably get people's impressions. You will need to have a facilitator for each group, and organizing and scheduling focus groups can take a lot of time. This information is subjective, and it could be time-consuming to compile the data.

CASE STUDIES

Use case studies to fully understand or depict a customer's experiences as a participant in your project's input, process, and results. This is a powerful way to portray to outsiders the impact your project has had on individuals, and it may be the best way to convey something like change in quality of life. Case studies are very time-consuming, and they are difficult to collect, organize, and describe.

Writing an Evaluation Plan

You can incorporate outcome-based evaluation into library planning and grant proposals by devising evaluation plans for your projects during the planning stage. This strategy naturally informs the library and community in measurable terms of the impact on customers as well as prepares the evaluation section of your grant application well before the deadline. Participants who follow this results-oriented approach to one particular library project will discover that although it may require more time, energy, and resources, it can lead to more focused and successful programs and services. Once an initial project has been designed and implemented in this fashion, the methodology can be applied to other library projects. And in the course of a few years, most of the significant projects will be measurable in terms of customer benefits.

The key to writing an evaluation plan is to first have objectives that are measurable; the two are intertwined. If the objectives are written in vague terms and can't be measured, the evaluation section will be vague and weak. With measurable objectives, the evaluation section will become a natural extension of the objectives and will be relatively easy to compose. It might help to think of objectives as the purpose of your project, the "things" that are left when the project is over. Usually, objectives are written in terms of increases and/or decreases.

For example, specific types of skills, such as problem solving, will show an increase while undesirable behaviors, such as truancy, will show a decrease. If you have worked through the project planning process to this point, you already have all the information you need to easily develop an evaluation plan. Figure 3.8 shows a sample evaluation plan for the Information at Your Fingertips project. Use the Evaluation Plan Worksheet provided in part III (see p. 181) and online (www.alaeditions.org/webextras) to develop your project evaluation plan.

KEY CONSIDERATIONS FOR WRITING AN EVALUATION PLAN

Consider the following key questions when you are designing a project evaluation:

- What is the purpose of the evaluation (i.e., what do you want to measure as a result of the evaluation)?
- Who are the audiences for the evaluation results or reports (e.g., funders, government, board, staff, partners, other libraries, and potential partners)?

- What kinds of information do you need to measure your progress, the strengths and weaknesses of the project, impact on customers, or how and why the project failed?
- What sources will you use to collect the information (e.g., staff, customers, program documentation)?
- How can the information be collected (e.g., questionnaires, interviews, observation, conducting focus groups)?
- When do you need the information?
- What resources are available to collect the information?

Now record your evaluation methods in #12 of your Project Planning Worksheet. Congratulations! Your project plan is complete.

FIGURE 3.8

SAMPLE EVALUATION PLAN: INFORMATION AT YOUR FINGERTIPS PROJECT

OBJECTIVE	EVALUATION METHOD	TIMELINE
By July 2018, there will be 25 percent more registered library cardholders in the three area codes with the greatest number of people who are Spanish speakers and members of the growing refugee population.	• Determine three area codes with the greatest number of Spanish speakers and refugees. • Generate and analyze cardholder data in the three area codes. • Create baseline and target numbers to equal 25 percent increase. • Determine percentage increase.	January–February July
By September 2018, 50 percent of the people in the target population who attend classes about how to find information online will say their knowledge increased.	• Conduct pre- and post-tests/surveys in class to determine participants' level of knowledge about how to find information online. This will be done prior to the taking of a class and at the conclusion of the class. • Conduct interviews with participants to evaluate what increased knowledge means in their lives.	May–September
By December 2018, 75 percent of the target population who use the library's website will say they had the ability to find the information they needed.	• Conduct interviews with representatives of the target population to determine website usability and their success in finding the information they need. • Conduct surveys of members of the target population as they leave the library's website to determine if they found the information they needed.	December
By December 2018, 25 percent of people in the community who speak Spanish or who are members of the growing refugee population will know how to find information in the library and online and know how to evaluate it.	• Conduct pre- and post-tests/surveys in class to determine participants' level of knowledge about how to find information online. This will be done prior to the taking of a class and at the conclusion of the class. • Conduct interviews with participants after the class to evaluate their confidence in finding reliable information that they need. • Prepare case studies.	July–December

Finding Library Funders

The previous chapters detailed the grant process and how to plan for success, including designing a specific project based on your community's needs. Now, let's explore different funding sources so that you can locate funders that have an interest in funding libraries and projects like yours.

Determining a Good Match

For successful grant matchmaking to occur, the library's mission and the goals of the grant project must complement those of the funding organization. A good match occurs when you can find aligned purposes. If you've followed the Grant Process Cycle, you've already done a lot of planning and determined your library's capacity for your grant project and how much funding you need to be successful. In the next chapter, we cover in-depth research of funders and how to discover their usual funding cycles, typical projects, and grant amounts through the use of databases, websites, and other resources, such as tax forms. It is important to establish your project goals, funding needs, and capacity *before* you look for funders so that you know what size grants and what types of funders will be the right fit for your current plans.

Remember that grant work is about people and developing relationships. The relationship you have with your funder will be very important. When we talk about funders and funding organizations, we sometimes forget that there are real people whom you can reach out to for guidance. As in any relationship, it is important to establish good communication practices from the start. Contacting a potential funder can be a start, as long as you've researched the organization and found out as much as you can about its grant programs beforehand. Then, if you have questions while writing the proposal, you will already have a contact and someone who knows about your grant project before the proposal submission process has even begun. Not all funders are easily approachable, but many have specific staff whose job it is to help grantees; examples include state libraries, state humanities councils, and both large and small foundations. Large federal funders, such as the Institute of Museum and Library Services (IMLS), sometimes hold webinars and will answer

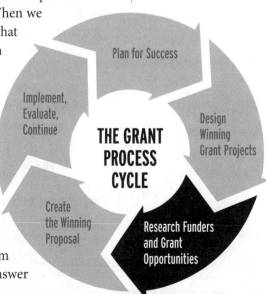

THE GRANT PROCESS CYCLE

Plan for Success

Design Winning Grant Projects

Research Funders and Grant Opportunities

Create the Winning Proposal

Implement, Evaluate, Continue

specific questions from potential grantees during that time. And after you are funded, remember to keep growing that relationship by thanking the funders, meeting reporting deadlines, and sending them any media coverage and other updates on your grant project.

For the purposes of this book, a "source" is the origin of the funding—the funder or grantor. Being familiar with the different types of sources for library grants can help ensure that your grant proposal reaches the right audience. The remainder of this chapter takes a closer look at the two major types of grant funding sources, government and private, and at the resources you can use to find the grant announcements. Within each type are several categories, as illustrated in figure 4.1.

FIGURE 4.1

TYPES OF FUNDING SOURCES

GOVERNMENT	PRIVATE
• Federal government • State government • Local government (county, city, town, village, municipality)	• Foundations and nonprofits • Corporations and corporate foundations • Clubs and organizations • Professional and trade associations

---

Government Funding for Libraries

Government grants can come from all levels of government: federal, state, or local (county, city, town, or village).

Federal Government Sources

The federal government is the largest source of grant funding in the United States, awarding billions of dollars annually for research and development, facilities improvement, demonstration projects, and model projects. Federal grants are given to carry out a broad range of educational and social reforms and initiatives for purposes established by federal legislation. The federal government issues two kinds of grants: (1) discretionary and (2) formula (or block) grants. Federal funding that is available directly from a federal agency or department is called a discretionary grant. Formula (or block) grants are federal funds passed on to states, counties, or local governments for distribution. Libraries can apply for either kind.

Each government department, bureau, or office has unique priorities and grant guidelines. There are hundreds of federal government grant programs managed by a wide variety of departmental bureaus. Grants from federal government agencies are highly competitive and they can be very complex. Federal grant proposals can be hundreds of pages long and require months of preparation.

The Internet is the most reliable source for locating federal government grant resources today. Grants.gov is the single free access point for over 1,000 grant programs offered by the twenty-six federal grant-making agencies. Search tips and resources for locating government grants are included in the next chapter.

Library-related grants are frequently given by the Institute of Museum and Library Services, the National Endowment for the Arts, the National Endowment for the Humanities, the National Library of Medicine, the Department of Housing and Urban Development Community Development Block Grant Program, and the U.S. Department of Education. The following U.S. federal government agencies all fund projects of interest to libraries, information clearinghouses, archives, technical information services, and their partners and collaborators.

U.S. Department of Agriculture (USDA)

The USDA (www.usda.gov) serves all Americans through anti-hunger efforts, through stewardship of nearly 200 million acres of national forest and rangelands, and through product safety and conservation efforts. Examples of recent programs open to libraries include these:

- *Rural Community Development Initiative (RCDI) Grants*: RCDI grants (www
  .rd.usda.gov/programs-services/rural-community-development-initiative
  -grants) have helped many rural libraries with improving and building new
  facilities.
- *Rural Broadband Access Loan and Loan Guarantee Program (Broadband
  Program)*: The Broadband Program (www.rd.usda.gov/programs-services/
  farm-bill-broadband-loans-loan-guarantees) furnishes loans and loan
  guarantees to provide funds for the costs of construction, improvement,
  or acquisition of facilities and equipment needed to provide service at the
  broadband lending speed in eligible rural areas.

U.S. Department of Education (ED)

The ED (www2.ed.gov/fund/grants-apply.html) administers a budget of $68 billion. ED's mission is to promote student achievement and preparation for global competitiveness by fostering educational excellence and ensuring equal access. The following ED offices administer grants of potential interest to libraries:

- *Institute of Education Sciences (IES)*: IES (www2.ed.gov/about/offices/list/ies)
  compiles statistics; funds research, evaluations, and information dissemination;
  and provides research-based guidance to further evidence-based policy and
  practice.
- *Office of Innovation and Improvement (OII)*: OII's (innovation.ed.gov) mission
  is to accelerate the pace at which the United States identifies, develops, and
  scales solutions to education's most important or persistent challenges. OII

makes strategic investments in innovative educational programs and practices and administers more than twenty-five discretionary grant programs managed by four program offices: Charter Schools Program, Parental Options and Improvement, Teacher Quality Programs, and the Office of Investing in Innovation.

- *Office of Elementary and Secondary Education (OESE)*: OESE (www2.ed .gov/about/offices/list/oese) provides financial assistance to state and local education agencies for both public and private preschool, elementary, and secondary education. Recent grant programs for school libraries include (1) Improving Literacy Through School Libraries, designed to improve the literacy skills and academic achievement of students by providing them with access to up-to-date school library materials, technologically advanced school library media centers, and professionally certified school library media specialists; and (2) Innovative Programs (Title V, Part A), with the purpose of improving the quality of education for all students through local education reform efforts that provide State Educational Agencies and Local Educational Agencies with an opportunity for innovation and educational improvement, including support programs to provide library services and instructional and media materials.
- *Office of English Language Acquisition (OELA)*: OELA (www2.ed.gov/about/ offices/list/oela) administers programs designed to enable students with limited English proficiency to become proficient in English and to meet challenging state academic content and student achievement standards.
- *Office of Postsecondary Education (OPE)*: OPE (www2.ed.gov/about/offices/ list/ope) directs, coordinates, and recommends policies for programs that are designed to provide financial assistance to eligible students, improve postsecondary educational facilities and programs, recruit and prepare disadvantaged students for postsecondary programs, and promote the domestic study of foreign languages and international affairs, research, and exchange activities.
- *Office of Special Education and Rehabilitative Services (OSERS)*: OSERS (www2.ed.gov/about/offices/list/osers) assists in the education of children with disabilities and the rehabilitation of adults with disabilities and conducts research to improve the lives of individuals with disabilities regardless of age.
- *Office of Career, Technical, and Adult Education (OCTAE)*: OCTAE (www2.ed .gov/about/offices/list/ovae) administers and coordinates programs that are related to adult education and literacy, career and technical education, and community colleges. This includes administering the Adult Education formula grant program to the states.

U.S. Department of Health and Human Services (HHS)

The mission of HHS (www.hhs.gov) is to enhance and protect the health and well-being of all Americans. The department fulfills its mission by providing for effective health and human services and fostering advances in medicine, public health, and social services.

HHS has eleven operating divisions, including eight agencies in the U.S. Public Health Service and three human services agencies. The following are a few of the agencies that provide funding for library grant projects:

- *Administration for Children and Families (ACF)*: ACF (www.acf.hhs.gov/ grants) is a federal agency funding state, territory, local, and tribal organizations to provide family assistance (welfare), child support, child care, Head Start, child welfare, and other programs relating to children and families. Actual services are provided by state, county, city, and tribal governments and public and private local agencies. ACF assists these organizations through funding, policy direction, and information services.
- *Health Resources and Services Administration (HRSA)*: HRSA (www.hrsa .gov/grants) makes grants to organizations to improve and expand health care services for underserved people. HRSA's programs are designed to increase access to care, improve quality, and safeguard the health and well-being of the nation's most vulnerable populations.
- *National Library of Medicine (NLM)*: As part of the National Institutes of Health, the NLM (www.nlm.nih.gov/grants.html) awards grants for research, resource development, training, career development and small business research and development. All NLM grants focus on the use of computers and information sciences to improve the access, storage, retrieval, management, dissemination, and use of biomedical information.
- *National Network of Libraries of Medicine (NN/LM)*: NN/LM (nnlm.gov/ funding) advances the progress of medicine and improves the public health by providing U.S. health professionals with equal access to biomedical information and improving the public's access to information to enable them to make informed decisions about their health. NN/LM is coordinated by the National Library of Medicine and carried out through a nationwide network of health science libraries and information centers. Grants are offered by each region in the network and focus on access to health information through outreach, professional development, technology, and training. Follow the links under Regional Funding Opportunities to find open opportunities for projects, including those related to health literacy training for librarians or the public, school/library partnerships, and librarian professional development.

U.S. Department of Housing and Urban Development (HUD)

HUD administers the Community Development Block Grant (CDBG) program (portal .hud.gov/hudportal/HUD?src=/program_offices/comm_planning/communitydevelop ment/programs). CDBG is a flexible program that provides communities with resources to address a wide range of unique community development needs, such as services to the most vulnerable in our communities, the creation of jobs through the expansion and retention of businesses, and projects related to infrastructure, installation and support of public facilities, and community centers.

U.S. Environmental Protection Agency (EPA)

The EPA (www.epa.gov/grants) has some grant programs applicable to library work:

- *Brownfields*: The Brownfields program (www.epa.gov/brownfields) empowers states, communities, and other stakeholders to work together to prevent, assess, safely clean up, and sustainably reuse brownfields. A brownfield site is real property, the expansion, redevelopment, or reuse of which may be complicated by the presence or potential presence of a hazardous substance, pollutant, or contaminant.
- *Green Building*: Numerous sources of funding for the Green Building program (www.epa.gov/greenbuilding/tools/funding.htm) are available at the national, state, and local levels for homeowners, industry, government organizations, and nonprofits.

U.S. Department of Justice, Office of Juvenile Justice and Delinquency Prevention (OJJDP)

OJJDP (www.ojjdp.gov/funding/funding.html) provides funding to states, territories, localities, and private organizations, including faith-based institutions, through formula and block grants and discretionary grants to prevent and respond to juvenile delinquency and victimization.

Institute of Museum and Library Services (IMLS)

IMLS (www.imls.gov) is the primary source of federal support for the nation's 122,000 libraries and 17,500 museums. The institute's mission is to create strong libraries and museums that connect people to information and ideas. IMLS grants are available for archives, federally recognized Native American tribes, historical societies, libraries, museums, nonprofits that serve Native Hawaiians, professional associations, regional organizations, state library administrative agencies, state or local governments, and public or private nonprofit institutions of higher education. Every year the IMLS allocates LSTA funding, using a population-based formula, to state library agencies for distribution to libraries throughout each state. (See State Library Agencies in the following section, State and Local Government Sources.)

National Endowment for the Arts (NEA)

NEA (www.arts.gov/grants) is a public agency dedicated to supporting excellence in the arts, bringing the arts to all Americans, and providing leadership in arts education. NEA is the nation's largest annual funder of the arts, bringing great art to all fifty states, including rural areas, inner cities, and military bases. Recent grant programs with successful library applicants include Big Read, Our Town, Art Works, and Challenge America.

National Endowment for the Humanities (NEH)

NEH (www.neh.gov/grants) is an independent grant-making agency of the U.S. government dedicated to supporting research, education, preservation, and public programs in the humanities. Recent grant programs applicable to libraries include Sustaining Cultural Heritage Collections, for planning and implementation of preservation projects; the National Digital Newspaper Program; and Digital Humanities Start-Up Grants, for planning digital projects.

National Historical Publications and Records Commission (NHPRC)

NHPRC (www.archives.gov/nhprc/announcement) is the grant-making affiliate of the U.S. National Archives and Records Administration (NARA). The NHPRC promotes the preservation and use of America's documentary heritage essential to understanding our democracy, history, and culture. Each year Congress appropriates up to $10 million for grants to support the nation's archives and for projects to edit and publish historical records of national importance. Recent grant opportunities for library projects include Access to Historical Records, to support archival repositories in preserving and processing primary source materials; Digital Dissemination of Archival Collections; and Public Engagement with Historical Records, to encourage citizen engagement with historical records.

Workforce Innovation and Opportunity Act (WIOA)

Originally known as the Workforce Investment Act, Congress reauthorized and renamed the act in 2014. WIOA (www.doleta.gov/wioa; see also www.ala.org/advocacy/advleg/federallegislation/workforce) helps job seekers and workers access employment, education, training, and support services to succeed in the labor market. This legislation recognizes the role that libraries serve for job seekers and that libraries should be integrated into state and local plans to deliver these crucial services. WIOA provides formula grants to states through the U.S. Department of Labor (DOL) and adult education and literacy programs and vocational rehabilitation state grant programs to assist individuals with disabilities in obtaining employment through the U.S. Department of Education (ED).

State and Local Government Sources

Some federal funding is passed directly to states, counties, or local governments for their use or for redistribution through formula (or block) grants to their jurisdictions. A state or local government entity may acquire a grant of its own that requires others to perform part of a project's scope of work. In this case, the local government will issue an RFP for services or products. Libraries may be eligible for a formula or block grant or may respond to an RFP to perform work on a state grant. The state grants you might be most familiar with are grants offered through state library agencies. State departments of education and state humanities, arts, and cultural agencies are also good sources for funding library projects. Look for RFPs or grant opportunities available on a competitive or noncompetitive basis.

Investigate grant opportunities available through state, county, or city agencies and departments by checking their websites regularly for RFPs and subgrant offerings. Make contact with key officials in departments that are likely to fund a project like yours, should they have funding. Ask to be notified if funding becomes available.

State Library Agencies

State library agencies are one example of a state government source that offers grants to libraries using federal funds received as formula grants. The primary example of library funding disbursed this way is LSTA funds, distributed by IMLS to state libraries (www .imls.gov/grants/grants-state/state-profiles). LSTA funding is the only federal funding exclusively for libraries.

The Grants to States program is the largest source of federal funding support for library services in the United States. Every year IMLS distributes more than $150 million in LSTA funding to the fifty-nine State Library Administrative Agencies (SLAAs) for distribution to libraries throughout each state using a population-based formula. SLAAs may use the funds to support statewide initiatives and services, and they may also distribute the funds through competitive subawards to, or cooperative agreements with, public, academic, research, school, or special libraries or consortia (for-profit and federal libraries are not eligible). LSTA guidelines specify that each state must develop goals and objectives for a five-year plan to strengthen the efficiency, reach, and effectiveness of library services in that state. State libraries then determine distribution of LSTA funds based on their individual states' areas of need and priorities.

LSTA funding has increased over the past several years and continues to be a good source of funding for most libraries. Funding for LSTA increased in fiscal year 2016 (FY16) to $183 million, more than the fiscal year 2015 (FY15) level of $181 million. Grants to States received an FY16 boost to $155.8 million ($154.8 million in FY15).

As LSTA funding continues to be a primary source of library grant funding, you should find out if your state library offers LSTA subgrants, state grants-in-aid, or other funding by checking its website. Many state libraries provide applications online, and some state libraries offer free grant workshops and/or support from staff. An added benefit to this state distribution of federal funding is that it is much easier to develop a relationship with state library personnel than with federal funders, plus the competition may not be as stiff. If you are applying on behalf of an academic or special library, you may need to partner with a public library to be eligible, depending on the requirements of your state library.

State Arts Agencies

State arts agencies increase public access to the arts and work to ensure that every community in America enjoys the cultural, civic, economic and educational benefits of a thriving arts sector.

Every state arts agency offers a unique combination of grants and services for artists, arts organizations, schools, and community groups. The directory of the National Assembly of State Arts Agencies (NASAA; www.nasaa-arts.org/About/State-Arts -Agency-Directory) has contact and website information. Taking the time to talk with your state arts agency's knowledgeable staff will start you on the path to applying for funding.

State Departments of Education

State departments of education give funding to states through formula grants, such as The Division of Adult Education and Literacy (DAEL) grants for adult education and literacy programs, and the 21st Century Community Learning Centers grants. The U.S. ED (www2.ed.gov/about/contacts/state/index.html) provides contact information for these state departments.

State Humanities Councils

The fifty-six humanities councils located in all U.S. states and jurisdictions support local humanities programs and events. The state humanities councils are funded in part by the federal government through NEH's Federal/State Partnership Office (www .neh.gov/about/state-humanities-councils). They also receive funding from private donations, foundations, corporations, and, in some cases, state governments. Many libraries report successful relationships with their state humanities councils through "mini-grants" or "resource grants" programs that support public humanities programs such as reading groups, lecture/discussion programs, traveling exhibits, book festivals, and humanities scholars.

Local Government Grants

Make sure that you have local government connections that can let you know about funding opportunities in your geographic area. To search for local opportunities, use your local or state funding directory (www.nal.usda.gov/ric/guide -to-funding-resources#internetdirectories). State libraries and college and university libraries generally provide these types of funding directories and research tools. Also contact your city and county government (https://www.usa.gov/local-governments). Depending on your grant project topic, you will want to reach out to your local departments of arts, business, community development, environment, historical preservation, education, youth, technology, and/or archives.

Private Funding for Libraries

While government grant resources are driven primarily by legislation, private grant resources have their own individual funding interests and priorities. Foundations, non-profits, businesses and corporations, clubs, and professional and trade associations are sources of private grants. They may be small organizations, staffed mostly with volunteers, or they may be large multimillion-dollar enterprises with many professional staff.

More information on researching private funding opportunities is included in the next chapter. Here are some top resources to start locating funders:

- The Grantsmanship Center maintains information about your state's foundations, community foundations, corporate giving programs and the top giving foundations in your state (www.tgci.com/funding-sources).
- Local community directories, yellow pages, and sites for community organizations that provide funding are valuable sources of information.
- The USDA maintains a list of state and local foundation directories (www.nal .usda.gov/ric/guide-to-funding-resources#internetdirectories).
- Michigan State University has an extensive list of service clubs and civic organizations that provide funding (http://staff.lib.msu.edu/harris23/grants/ servicec.htm).
- Your library board, Friends group, and staff may also help identify local clubs and organizations that provide funding.
- One of the best ways to find out about these private funding opportunities is through local websites or by contacting the organizations directly.

Foundations

Foundations support the specific ideals that inspired their creation. Billions of dollars are granted annually by foundations to help libraries, schools, communities, and other nonprofit organizations reach their goals. The majority of U.S. grant-giving foundations are required by law to distribute 5 percent of their investment assets annually for charitable purposes.

There are very large foundations and corporations that provide annual funding opportunities. These are often very competitive, so also look for local foundation opportunities by connecting with fundraising and philanthropy networks in your own region. Local grants can be less competitive, and the organizations will likely be focused on supporting their own communities.

There are three main kinds of foundations:

- *Independent foundations* are created by an individual or a family, often through endowment funds, and are the most common type of private foundation. Grants may be legally mandated by the foundation donor to restrict funding to specific causes or to geographical regions.
- *Corporate foundations* are funded and created by companies and are legal entities that are operated by a board of directors. They may have national or

local giving programs, and some have both national grant programs as well as local giving opportunities.

- *Community/public foundations* are publicly supported foundations that operate for the benefit of a specific geographic region. Assets are received from many individual donors and diverse sources. Individual donors can establish endowed funds without the costs of starting their own foundations. These institutions are governed by volunteer boards of community leaders and administered by full-time professional staff with expertise in knowing their communities' needs. They are often cited as one of the fastest-growing sectors of philanthropy in the United States. There are over 700 community foundations with assets of approximately $55 billion, awarding grants of more than $4.2 billion each year. Community foundations have resource materials, local directories, and more information about funding opportunities in your area. Use the Council on Foundations' Community Foundation Locator (www.cof.org/community-foundation-locator) to locate community foundations near you.

Corporate Funding Sources

Corporations often create corporate foundations for the purpose of granting money for specific projects or areas of interest. Corporations offer many opportunities in the form of partnerships, material resources, mentors, expertise, and funds to schools, communities, libraries, and other nonprofits. Corporations are generally interested in establishing their names and relationships within the communities in which they operate. You may find annual reports or other compilations that include descriptions of the corporations' granting interests and grant-making history. Don't forget to check local finding directories specific to your state or geographical region for corporate funding opportunities. Check foundation resources for corporate foundations as well as the resources in the next chapter, such as the *National Directory of Corporate Giving* (from the Foundation Center) and the *Corporate Giving Directory* (from Information Today), for additional corporate foundations and corporate direct giving programs.

Professional Associations

Professional associations often make grant funds available to members of their associations or to other organizations that carry out missions that are compatible with the interests of the professional associations.

Investigate your state, regional, and special library associations, including divisions, special interest groups, chapters, and library foundations. The American Library Association (ALA), Public Library Association (PLA), and American Association of School Librarians (AASL) offer many grant, award, scholarship, and fellowship opportunities. Check your professional associations' websites for grant funding that is available for members and join their electronic discussion groups.

The following divisions of ALA may have grants available; all opportunities are listed on the ALA "Awards, Grants, and Scholarships" webpage (www.ala.org/awardsgrants):

- American Association of School Librarians (AASL)
- Association for Library Collections & Technical Services (ALCTS)
- Association for Library Service to Children (ALSC)
- Association of College & Research Libraries (ACRL)
- Association of Specialized & Cooperative Library Agencies (ASCLA)
- Library Information Technology Association (LITA)
- Library Leadership & Management Association (LLAMA)
- Public Library Association (PLA)
- Reference & User Services Association (RUSA)
- United for Libraries
- Young Adult Library Services Association (YALSA)

Finding Local Funding Sources

Local research may require personal communication, such as phone calls, networking, relationship building, and marketing your project idea. Here are some places for you to start your local research.

Local Clubs and Organizations

Clubs and organizations may have a service, civic, or skills-based focus and provide support for local projects and programs. They usually have local chapters, such as the Lions Club, Rotary, Association of Junior Leagues, Kiwanis, Civitan, and Elks. These local-funding opportunities are usually not widely advertised or promoted. This is where your networking and people skills will come in handy. Ask library staff, library Friends members, and board members to help identify local clubs and organizations that provide funding. Your own friends and family members who are involved in local organizations can also tell you what their organizations support. Mention your idea or project to them and inquire about the possibility of presenting it to their organizations. Ask if they know any other local organizations that support ideas or projects like yours.

Local Businesses

Visit your local community foundation and chamber of commerce and ask to see the information they have about businesses or corporations in your area that fund local projects. Some corporations have national giving programs but also local community-oriented grants. Some are required to give funds locally every month.

Look at local business websites for information about their community involvement. Talk to local banks and stores to find out if they have giving programs. Ask your board for help in connecting with potential business funders in your community. Watch the local newspaper for articles about grants given to other nonprofits in your community and follow up with the funders.

Also, large chain stores will have grants that are available for local funding. Here are a few sources to check out in your area that have given local grants to other libraries:

- Banks
- Grocery stores
- Insurance companies
- Drugstores
- Restaurants
- Technology stores (such as Best Buy)
- Utility companies
- Target
- Dollar General
- Walmart
- Build-A-Bear

The next chapter provides tips and techniques for researching funders and top resources for all kinds of funding opportunities.

Researching and Selecting the Right Grant Opportunity

Now that you understand how to plan a grant project and know about the different library funding sources, it is time to do further research and select the funders that will support projects just like yours. We close the chapter with tips for staying aware of new grant opportunities and talking with funders.

It's both the good news but also the bad news: there are *a lot* of grant opportunities out there! So what should you do to make sure you find the *right funder* with the *right grant* for your library project? Here are some tips for you to think about while you do your research.

Research Tips and Techniques

Do the Research

Grant research is usually the easy part for librarians. We have an advantage when it comes to doing grant research because we are trained to effectively use reference materials and electronic resources. Not only do we have the skills it takes to find information; we are a persistent group who will find information wherever it may be and however deeply it is buried. We're naturals. So, let's put our valuable information-finding skills to work and find the grant that will fund our projects to meet the needs of our communities.

Use the Language of the Resources and Funders

When identifying keywords describing your project, remove any mental barriers you may have about libraries and what librarians traditionally do. Eliminate stereotypes and think big. Be generous and open-minded about choosing terms, and avoid narrowly defining your project for now. Funders and resource compilers may not even think of libraries when they are writing profiles, defining areas of focus, or composing calls for proposals. Refrain

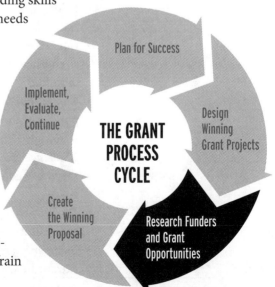

THE GRANT PROCESS CYCLE

Plan for Success

Design Winning Grant Projects

Research Funders and Grant Opportunities

Create the Winning Proposal

Implement, Evaluate, Continue

from using "library-speak," and think broadly. For instance, if a funder is interested in awarding grants for children's performances, the funder may not know many libraries would be interested in this opportunity. In a case like this, "library" would not appear as a keyword in the entry, but "children," "theater," and "performance art" would. If you search only for "library" or "library theater," you will miss this potential funder. Make sure to uncover every possible match by thinking broadly when it comes to keywords describing your project. Include synonyms, alternate spellings, and multiple terms with similar meanings.

Stay in this frame of mind when you are deciding which resources to search. Of course, you will want to use library-specific resources like *The ALA Book of Library Grant Money*, Ninth Edition, edited by Nancy Kalikow Maxell (2014), and the *Library Grants* blog (http://librarygrants.blogspot.com). However, don't overlook other subject guides, such as those from the Foundation Center: *Grants for Arts, Culture, and the Humanities* is helpful if your project involves an art exhibit, humanities program, or cultural performance. Consult *Grants for People with Disabilities* or *Grants for Children and Youth* if your project will serve those target audiences. Thoroughly search for local or lesser-known specific funding resources that may help you in your search for a grant.

Spend some time examining each resource to understand the unique terms used in the resource and how the resource defines terms. Definitions are usually included in a glossary, appendix, or user's guide. Learn how a resource defines different kinds of grants and use exactly those terms to narrow your search.

Understand the Different Kinds of Grants

Before you begin your research, familiarize yourself with the terminology used for different kinds of grants. If you understand what these kinds of grants fund, you will save yourself time by researching only grants that are appropriate for your project and your library.

- *Block grant*: This is a federal grant awarded to state or local governments for a specific need or issue. Local and state governments then set specific grant guidelines within their own jurisdictions and make smaller grants to local agencies and nonprofits.
- *Capacity-building grant*: This type of grant helps agencies and nonprofits strengthen their internal operations so that they can be more effective/efficient in fulfilling their missions.
- *Capital-building grant*: This "bricks and mortar" funding grant is used to purchase land and construct, renovate, or rehabilitate buildings and facilities. It may also fund major equipment purchases or endowments.
- *Challenge grant*: This is a grant promised to awardees on the condition that they raise additional funds from other sources to reach a specific fundraising goal.
- *Discretionary grant*: This federal or state grant is awarded directly to community organizations, schools, and/or local governments.
- *Emergency grant*: This type of grant is made to help an agency through an extraordinary short-term or unexpected financial crisis.

- *Formula grant*: This noncompetitive grant is awarded by federal or state governments to lower levels of government based on a predetermined formula to address specific needs.
- *General operating support grant*: Funding from this grant is used for the general purpose or work of an organization, such as personnel, administration, and other expenses for an existing program.
- *Matching grant*: This grant requires awardees to provide a certain amount and funders to provide the rest. For example, a 1:1 match means that the funder and the library each provide half of the cost of the project.
- *Project/program grant*: Funding from this grant is for a specific initiative or new endeavor, not for general purposes.
- *Research grant*: This grant supports a specific research project or issue.
- *Seed grant*: Funding from this grant is designed to help start a new project or charitable activity or to help a new organization in its start-up phase.
- *Technology grant*: This grant provides funding for a technology project, including equipment.

Begin with Broad Searches and Narrow to the Specific

Broad Research

To begin your research, develop a list of keywords that describe your project. A good way to do this is by recording the goals, objectives, and activities of your grant project on our Keyword Selection Worksheet, provided in part III (see p. 182) and online (www .alaeditions.org/webextras). You can take this information directly from your Project Planning Worksheet, if you completed it as part of chapter 3. Think of broad, narrow, and related terms, and don't forget to include variations on words and synonyms. Start with general keywords like "library," "libraries," or "information." Then think of words more specific to your project yet still broad, like "technology," "resources," "services," or "instruction."

You can even do a team brainstorming activity or work in small groups to develop a comprehensive list of keywords that describe your project. Team members might be given ten minutes to write down keywords on their own Keyword Selection Worksheets first. Record the keywords your team selects on one Keyword Selection Worksheet that you will use throughout your grant research to keep you on track and headed in the right direction. Figure 5.1 shows an example of a completed Keyword Selection Worksheet for the Information at Your Fingertips project that we designed in chapter 3.

Use these keywords to do your broad research in all the general resources appropriate for your project, such as national directories and grants databases for government, foundation, corporate, and local funders.

Narrowing Your Search

As you narrow your research, you will use more specific resources, such as electronic databases, local directories, and subject directories. Databases and websites often allow

FIGURE 5.1

SAMPLE KEYWORD SELECTION WORKSHEET

PROJECT PLAN	KEYWORDS
Goals 1. Diverse community members will easily find and evaluate information they need using the library's resources and database, and other online resources. 2. The library is responsive to the changing information needs of diverse populations in our community. 3. The library successfully serves diverse communities in the library and on the library's website. **Objectives** 1. By July 2018, there will be 25 percent more registered library cardholders in the three area codes with the greatest number of people who are Spanish speakers and members of the growing refugee population. 2. By September 2018, 50 percent of the people in the target population who attend classes about how to find information online will say their knowledge increased. 3. By December 2018, 75 percent of the target population who use the library's website will say they had the ability to find the information they needed. 4. By December 2018, 25 percent of people in the community who speak Spanish or who are members of the growing refugee population will know how to find information in the library and online and how to evaluate it. **Outcomes** 1. Knowing how to use the library or library's website to find information will increase the ability of Spanish-speaking community members and people from foreign countries to make informed choices. 2. Community members who are from foreign countries and/or whose first language is not English will know about the information technology available in the library, and they will know how to use it to improve their quality of life. 3. As a result of library programs and seminars designed to meet their needs, Spanish-speaking community members and newly arrived refugees will gain knowledge that will help improve their life condition. **Activities and Action Steps** • Create brochures, flyers, and website banners to advertise. • Conduct needs assessments and focus groups. • Determine the location with the most people in the target population and generate data. • Hold public awareness campaigns and register new users. • Develop curricula. • Develop online tutorial.	• Adults • Community • Digital literacy • Diversity • Spanish • ESL • Computers • Learning • Seniors • Online • Tutorials • Website • Online • Outreach • Library • Public awareness • Refugees • Classes • Training • Information evaluation

you to combine multiple fields in one search, and they often will provide more in-depth information about targeted funding sources. Make yourself aware of what is available in the various resources you are using, and take full advantage of the information provided. Local funding directories list funders that limit their grant giving to your geographic area, as well as local corporate giving programs and small corporate grants that may not appear in the national directories. Likewise, subject directories may include funding sources just right for your project that may not be included in the national directories due to their size. In narrowing your search, you will begin to see some real funding possibilities. This part of your research can be time-consuming; don't rush it because this is where you will find the right funder for your project.

As you examine the funder entries in the broad research resources, compare your project keywords on the Keyword Selection Worksheet with a potential funder's purpose, field of interest or focus, and the type of support given. Decide whether a funder is a good match based on how relevant the information in the entries is to your project.

Record Your Findings

When you identify a likely funder, record the information about the funder on the Funder Summary Worksheet provided in part III (see p. 183) and online (www .alaeditions.org/webextras), in a spreadsheet, or using whatever method works best for you. Don't scrutinize too much at this point; make a worksheet for any funder that is a possibility. You could print out the individual worksheets and start a binder or save them to a computer folder that you can share with other team members. If you do this faithfully during the course of your research, when you finish, you will have a nice collection of Funder Summary Worksheets full of important information about funders that are potential matches for your grant project. These worksheets hold your research notes, providing the information you will need to move ahead while reducing the chance that you will miss some vital information you forgot to write down.

Organize Your Research

Keep your research organized by prioritizing your potential funders. You may determine that some are not good matches after all, or you may have questions on others. If you have questions on some opportunities or need further clarification on whether a funder may be interested in a project like yours, contact the funder. By now you should be very familiar with the foundation, agency, or corporation; therefore, you will be asking intelligent, informed questions. Use this initial contact to develop a rapport with the contact person. He or she is usually happy to answer your questions and work with you and will be pleasantly surprised at how much you already know from the research you have done. After this contact, you will know whether to keep this funder as a potential match for your project.

You can organize this information in a "low tech" way or by using grant management software. If you are going "low tech," file away funders that may be a good fit in the future using either paper folders or electronic files. Start a separate file for each potential funder. In each file, you can keep the worksheet and a record of contacts, phone notes, correspondence, and grant announcements. You can also share this information with others on your grant team using Dropbox, Google Docs, or other file-sharing methods your library has in place.

The work of tracking funders, preparing for grant proposal submissions, finding funding opportunities, and managing grant projects does take a good deal of collaboration and organization. There are grant management software platforms, for a "higher tech" approach, that offer solutions to make this process easier, including compiling grant opportunities, providing a way to vote on which opportunities to apply for, and communicating with other grant team members. Here are two online sources that provide reviews of grant management software:

- "Choose the Right Donor Management Software through TechSoup: Find Out Which Tool Is Right for Your Organization": The software programs included in this article are all available to libraries through TechSoup's Technology Donation Program (www.techsoup.org/support/articles-and-how-tos/choose -the-right-donor-management-software-through-techsoup).
- *A Consumers Guide to Donor Management Systems.* Idealware provides a detailed comparison report of donor management tools, most of which are also available through TechSoup's Library Donation Program (www.idealware.org/ reports/consumers-guide-donor-management-systems).

Systems that include donor management solutions will help with all aspects of your relationships with funders, including tracking how much you've raised, organizing all the useful information you know about your donors, managing mailings, sending e-mails, and printing reports on all this information. There are many systems available, ranging from the basic to the more complex. Costs vary as well, and there are systems for very limited budgets. Some libraries use the eCivis Grants Network, which is a grant management software used by state, local, and tribal governments to address every stage of the grant cycle that may be available for your use.

Talk about It!

Tell everyone you know, including library staff, board members, and volunteers, that you are seeking funding and give them an overview of your grant project. Approach potential partners and your local and state government officials to let them know about your search. Ask other libraries in your area about the grants they have received and who funded them. Talk to your relatives, your friends, and leaders in your community.

Plan to visit your chamber of commerce and community foundations and tell them about your project. Speak at local clubs and organizations about your grant projects and your search for funding. You never know who might be on a foundation's board or know someone who is a board member for a foundation that has just the right funding for your project. It can be surprising to find out who may know about potential funding for your project.

Top Resources for Finding Grant Opportunities

You will use many resources in your grant research because there is not one print directory, website, or database that will neatly list all the grants that match your specific project. Being familiar with the myriad resources and where to find the opportunities is the key to finding a grant that matches your project. We have compiled the top resources into the Winning Grants Sources and Resources Handout, available in part III (see p. 184) and online (www.alaeditions.org/webextras).

Some resources are costly, however. State libraries and college and university libraries generally provide funding directories and research tools. Look for a state-specific or a community-specific funding directory or database for your area because these local resources often contain opportunities you will not find in the national directories. Community foundations and local United Ways will have many resources. The Council on Foundations website (www.cof.org) contains many of these listings. These community foundations may have websites, grant newsletters, and other publications of specific interest to your local area. In each state, there is an office that regulates charities. In California, for example, it is the Registry of Charitable Trusts. Call or access your state office's website to see if it has publications and guides on your state funders.

The resources or tools you will use to identify funding opportunities are available in a variety of formats. Grant opportunities are compiled and listed in print directories, online databases, websites, print and electronic newsletters, and e-mail discussion groups. Here we provide a general overview of the available resources; however, remember that there may be resources specific to the topic of your project or your geographical region that are beyond the scope of this overview. You must do the research necessary to uncover these resources.

General Print Resources

- *The ALA Book of Library Grant Money*, Ninth Edition, edited by Nancy Kalikow Maxwell (2014) contains summary information on the major U.S. funding organizations supporting libraries and includes both private and government sources. Remember to consult other subject-specific directories that match your project, such as arts and culture, children and youth, health, and education.
- *Annual Register of Grant Support: A Directory of Funding Sources*, published annually by Information Today (http://books.infotoday.com/directories/anreg .shtml), is a comprehensive directory that provides details on more than 3,000 major grant programs offered by traditional corporate, private, and public funding programs as well as lesser-known nontraditional grant sources, such as educational associations and unions.

Top Ten Online Sources for Finding Grant Opportunities

1. Foundation Center, http://foundationcenter.org/findfunders
2. The Grantsmanship Center, www.tgci.com/funding-sources
3. Grants.gov, www.grants.gov
4. Institute of Museum and Library Services, www.imls.gov/grants/apply-grant/available-grants
5. National Endowment for the Humanities, www.neh.gov/grants
6. National Network of Libraries of Medicine, nnlm.gov/funding
7. U.S. Department of Education, www2.ed.gov/fund/landing.jhtml?src=rt
8. IMLS, "State Profiles," www.imls.gov/grants/grants-state/state-profiles
9. *Library Grants* blog, http://librarygrants.blogspot.com
10. Google.com (It doesn't hurt to search for your grant project keywords to see what you find.)

We previously mentioned that local grants can be less competitive, thus easier to obtain. Even small grants can be worth the effort if they fit your project scope and intent better. Grants from local funders may have fewer strings attached than those from larger private or government agencies. You could also apply for several small grants that in combination could fund all the facets of a larger project.

A shortcut to finding library grants is available on a free website that we have coauthored since 2005, the *Library Grants* blog (http://librarygrants.blogspot.com). We post new grants every month and include the deadline, a brief description, and a link to more information. To save you time in your grant seeking, we verify that libraries of some type are eligible to apply for every grant opportunity. We include only national or large regional grants, so remember that there are also many local grants for you to explore. Reading our blog is a great way to get started looking for grants and to get an idea about what kinds of grants are out there and what funders are looking for. We focus on grants of interest to a national audience, updating the listing often, so that what you find there will be grants that are currently open. Follow the links in our postings to the actual grant announcements, application guidelines, and eligibility requirements. Visit the blog or subscribe to the RSS feed to be notified about grants as soon as we find out about them.

Researching Government Grant Resources

You can find all federal grant opportunities online through multiple locations.

Federal Agency Websites

Most federal agencies devote a section on their websites for announcing currently available grants. Look for a button near the top of the agency's home page labeled "Grants" or "Grant Applicants," or perform a search for "Grants" using the site's search box. See the previous chapter for a list of federal agencies with funding for libraries. These are some of the federal agencies that often post library grants:

- Institute of Museum and Library Services
- National Endowment for the Arts
- National Endowment for the Humanities
- National Library of Medicine
- U.S. Department of Education

Grants.gov

Grants.gov (www.grants.gov) is the centralized website for information on all annual grant funds available through the federal government. There are more than 1,000 grant programs, providing access to approximately $500 billion in annual awards. Here you can electronically find and apply for competitive grant opportunities from all twenty-six federal grant-making agencies. Grants.gov also supports electronic applications that can be downloaded and provides online user support tools and personalized assistance. You can sign up for an e-mail subscription service (www.grants.gov/search/subscribeAdvanced.do) that will notify you of new grant opportunities, and you can specify criteria, such as category of funding, eligibility, or agency. The site also offers RSS feeds (www.grants.gov/web/grants/rss.html).

Grants.gov is your best bet for an initial broad search for federal grants awarded directly to community agencies and organizations, schools, and libraries. To search for a grant opportunity, you do not need to register at the site; however, if you want to apply for a grant, you must register. This can take three to five business days, so if you think you might be applying, register early. For help with searching Grants.gov, check out the *Online User Guide* (www.grants.gov/help/html/help/index.htm).

There are three main options for searching for funding opportunities:

- *Home page search*: The home page includes four tabs under Find Open Grant Opportunities: (1) Newest Opportunities, (2) Browse Categories, (3) Browse Agencies, or (4) Browse Eligibilities.
- *Search Grants tab*: Click this tab at the top of the home page to access the keyword search and faceted search options.
- *Get a specific application package*: If you know the *CFDA* (*Catalog of Federal Domestic Assistance*) number or Funding Opportunity Number (FON) for a specific funding opportunity, use this process: (1) from the Applicants tab menu, click the Apply for Grants link; (2) click the Get Application Package button; (3) enter the *CFDA* number or FON; (4) click the Search button; (5) in the search results, click the FON link to access the View Grant Opportunity page for the funding opportunity you wish to download.

Go to the main Grants.gov page and click on the Search Grants tab to access the Grants .gov main search screen (see figure 5.2). You can do a basic search by keyword, FON, or *CFDA* number. You can also use the faceted search options to narrow your results.

Just click the appropriate facets on the left side of the "Search Grants" page to refine your search results. Facets are the different categories and options you can check and uncheck to narrow your existing search results. For example, you can limit your search by selecting your Eligibility based on whether your library is considered a government agency, a tribal organization, or a nonprofit. Or you can limit by Category, such as arts, humanities, or education (or whichever best matches your grant project or library emphasis). You can also limit by Agency, such as IMLS, NEH, or NEA. The other available facets are Opportunity Status and Funding Instrument Type. For a list of operators you can use to assist in your search, click on the Search Tips link in the upper right corner of the "Search Grants" page. You will be directed to the keyword "Search Tips" page.

Using the Basic Search Criteria fields, enter broad keyword terms in the Keyword(s) search box. Then click the Search tab and take a look at the results (see figure 5.2). Take note of the Close Date column. The deadlines for many grants in your results list may have already closed. Clicking on the Close Date column will arrange your results by closing date in descending order, thereby showing the open opportunities at the top of your list. From your results list, using any search mode on Grants.gov, you can click through to the original.

FIGURE 5.2

GRANTS.GOV SEARCH SCREEN

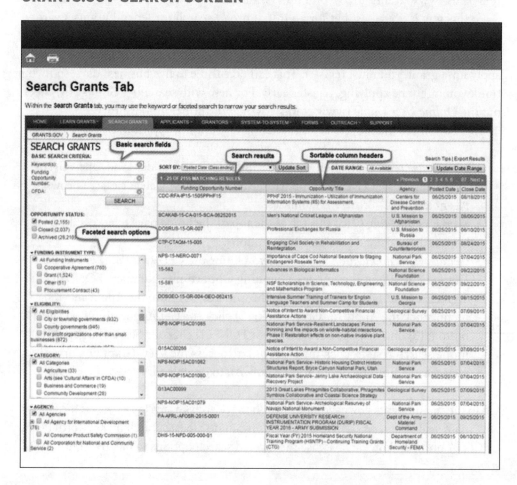

The basic keyword search searches grant titles and synopses only. If you aren't satisfied with your results, then from the main search page, you can select Browse Categories or Browse Agencies to do your broad search. When you use either of these options, your results list will be shorter and easier to browse; however, you may miss an opportunity offered by an agency or a category you inadvertently overlooked.

When you use Browse Agencies, remember to look at all the federal government agencies that fund libraries, clearinghouses, archives, and technical information services mentioned in chapter 4, such as the Department of Education, Department of Health and Human Services, National Endowment for the Arts, National Endowment for the Humanities, and the Institute of Museum and Library Services. Most of these agencies, such as IMLS, have their own websites (see figure 5.3) where they post the availability of grants, including guidelines as well as application and deadline information. Often, departmental websites offer more functionality for searching their grant opportunities. For instance, the IMLS site can be searched for available grants by grant name, institution, or project type.

FIGURE 5.3

IMLS WEBSITE

To narrow your search on Grants.gov, combine multiple fields such as title keywords, dates, funding activity categories, funding instrument types, eligibility, agencies, and subagencies (see figure 5.4). You can also limit your search to Opportunity Status: Posted, which is a big plus in narrowing your results to just those grants that are currently open for submissions.

FIGURE 5.4

GRANTS.GOV EXAMPLE SEARCH

By clicking on a Funding Opportunity Number link in the "Search Grants" results, you can find detailed information about the grant. The "View Grant Opportunity" page separates this information into four tabs: Synopsis, Version History, Related Documents, and Package. On each page for each of these tabs, you have the ability to review and print the opportunity information. The Package tab contains the links through which you will apply for the grant. Here, the Workspace Compatible column indicates whether each package is available through Workspace, a shared, online environment to apply through Grants.gov, which is helpful if more than one person is working on the grant application. For more information about Workspace, refer to the Manage My Workspaces help section of the Grants.gov *Online User Guide* (www.grants.gov/help/html/help/index.htm#t=Manage_My _Workspaces%2FManage_My_Workspaces.htm).

Federal Register

The *Federal Register* (www.federalregister.gov) is the official daily journal of U.S. federal agency information, including notifications and announcements of grant opportunities by federal agencies and organizations. Some federal grant opportunities appear in the *Federal Register* in the form of Notices of Funding Availability (NOFAs), Notices Inviting Applications, or Notices and Requests for Applications. A NOFA lists the application deadlines, priorities, eligibility requirements, and places where you can get more help in applying for program funds. Because some agencies have discontinued NOFAs in the *Federal Register*, also check the websites of federal agencies for available grants and full information.

To search for these announcements, start at the *Federal Register* main page, click the Browse tab at the top of the page, and then click on Topics in the drop-down menu. You can then browse by Grant programs or other specific grant program categories (e.g., Grant programs–education or Grant programs–housing and community development or Grant programs–social programs). You could click on the Search tab and go to Advanced Document Search and then check the boxes for (1) Publication Date (could limit by the current year or by a date range from three to six months ago to the present date) and (2) Notice, located under Document Category. You can limit by inclusive dates to narrow your search; however, be careful with this. You don't want to limit too narrowly and miss finding applicable grants. The periods of time between notice announcements and submission deadlines vary widely among federal agencies. Enter your broad keywords in the Find box, and add the truncated keyword "fund*" to include funds, funding, and other variations on the word. For more information, click on Learn More under the main Find box for information on Boolean searching capabilities and truncation.

Remember, you are starting with a broad search, so your results may require major sifting. The good news here is that you may catch something that wouldn't appear if you had performed a narrow search first. The extra work up front is sometimes worth it in the long run. If your broad search yields an overwhelming amount of results, begin to narrow your search with additional keywords until your results list is manageable. Figure 5.5 illustrates the search results.

When you click on an entry, you will go straight to the corresponding *Federal Register* announcement. See figure 5.6 for a sample *Federal Register* entry for an opportunity included in the results from the search illustrated in figure 5.5. As you will see, the notice provides complete information, including eligibility information, priorities, application and submission information, application review information, definitions, and whom to contact if you have questions.

FIGURE 5.5

FIGURE 5.5

FEDERAL REGISTER SEARCH

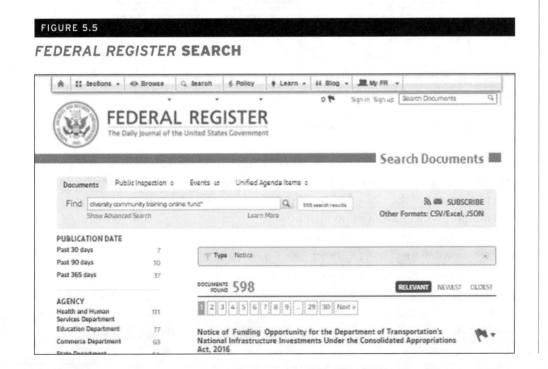

FIGURE 5.6

FEDERAL REGISTER GRANT ANNOUNCEMENT

The *Catalog of Federal Domestic Assistance (CFDA)*

The *CFDA* (www.cfda.gov) provides a full listing of all federal programs available to state and local governments; federally recognized Indian tribal governments; territories and possessions of the United States; domestic public, quasi-public, and private profit and nonprofit organizations and institutions; specialized groups; and individuals. The *CFDA* is disseminated electronically via its website, but a printable version is also available for downloading. There is also a *User Guide*, available in PDF format on the home page or from a link at the bottom of every page.

There are many ways to navigate the *CFDA* website. One way is to use the Find Programs search area on the right-hand side of the main page. Enter your keywords, select Project Grants under Assistance Type, and click on Search (see figure 5.7).

FIGURE 5.7

CFDA **SEARCH**

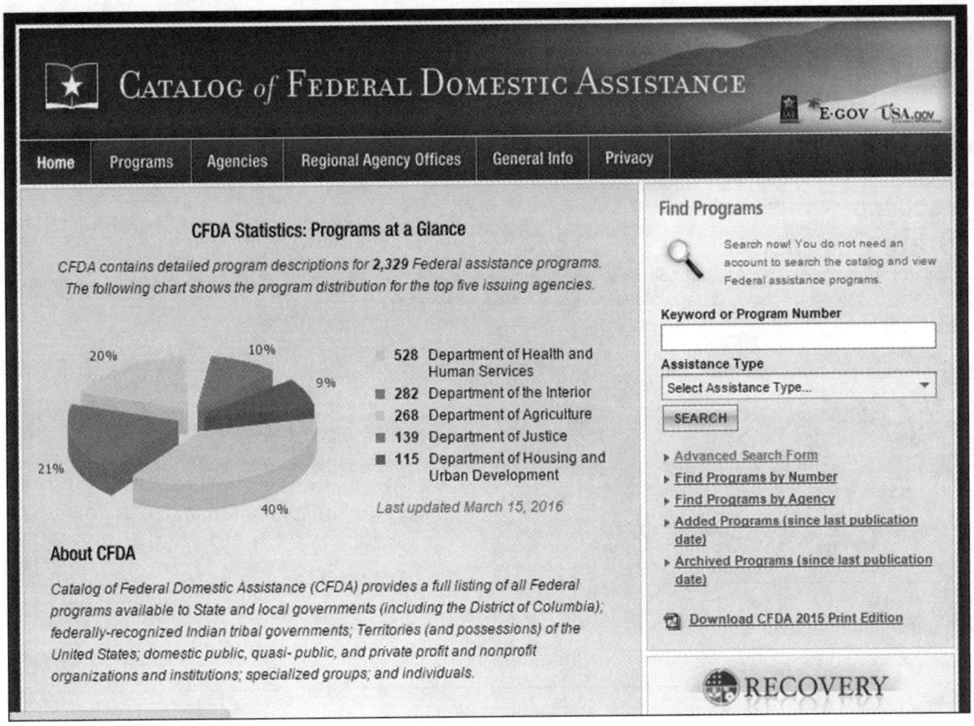

Figure 5.7 shows a list of all federal programs that fund project grants and contain the entered keywords. Be aware that these are not all active grant opportunities. You will be able to access information about a program on the *CFDA* site; however, to find out if a grant is currently available for the program, you must click through to the agency website.

The *CFDA* site is a good place to get an overall "big picture" view of federally funded grant programs in your area of interest. If you see a potential match that is not an active grant program, you can watch for an announcement on the *Federal Register* website, sign up for an e-mail alert on Grants.gov (www.grants.gov/search/subscribeAdvanced .do), or periodically revisit that agency's website for new grant announcements.

At the *CFDA* website you can search for formula grants, which are grants that funnel funds through state agencies. If you see a potential formula grant opportunity, follow through by contacting your state agency to inquire about applying for these funds. Using the Advanced Search form, you can narrow your search by functional area, agency and subagency, applicant and beneficiary eligibility, deadlines, type of assistance, and more.

State and Local Government Grant Resources

Some federal funding is passed directly to states, counties, or local governments for their use or for redistribution through formula (or block) grants. A state or city/local government entity may acquire a grant that requires others to perform part of a project's

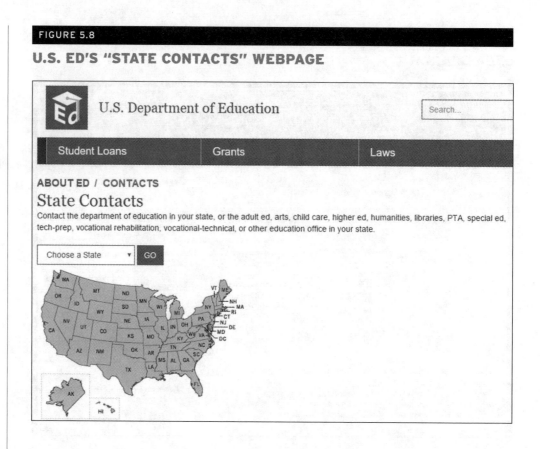

FIGURE 5.8

U.S. ED'S "STATE CONTACTS" WEBPAGE

scope of work. In this case, the local government will issue an RFP for services or products. Libraries may be eligible for a formula or block grant, or they may respond to an RFP to perform work on a state formula or block grant. Make sure that you have local government connections that can let you know about these local funding opportunities. One good source for county grants, if you are a member, is the National Association of Counties (NACo) Grants Clearinghouse (http://nacogrants.org). State departments of education (see figure 5.8) and state humanities (see figure 5.9), arts (see figure 5.10), and cultural agencies are also good sources for funding for library projects. Look for RFPs or grant opportunities available on a competitive or noncompetitive basis.

Researching Private Grant Resources

A nonprofit legally established in any state must obtain recognition as a charitable organization from the IRS so that contributions can be tax deductible. Most foundations apply for this 501(c)(3) status. The IRS requires foundations to make their information available by filing a Form 990. This form becomes a great source of information to the grant seeker, as it provides information about the foundation's finances, the grants it gives, and who serves as board members, for example. Both Form 990, for public charities, such as nonprofits and community foundations, and Form 990-PF, for private foundations, can be searched at the Foundation Center's

FIGURE 5.9

LOGOS OF STATE HUMANITIES COUNCILS

Logos of the 56 state and jurisdictional humanities councils, 2012. Click on image to enlarge.

Assembled from state humanities council information by Meg Ferris, Federal/State Partnership

FIGURE 5.10

NASAA'S "STATE ARTS AGENCY DIRECTORY" WEBPAGE

990 Finder (http://foundationcenter.org/findfunders/990finder). GuideStar (www .guidestar.org) also provides Form 990s for many tax-exempt organizations.

Websites of the foundations themselves are excellent sources of current information about a foundation, including its mission, what it is interested in funding, upcoming deadlines, application guidelines, recently funded projects, and contact information. You can find links to foundations by searching for a foundation on the Foundation Center's (http://foundationcenter.org) main page.

Foundation Resources

There are large foundations and corporations that have annual opportunities. These may be very competitive, so also look for local foundation opportunities by connecting with fundraising and philanthropy networks in your own region. Local grant opportunities can be less competitive, and the organizations will be especially interested in supporting your community.

In your search for foundations whose priorities align with your grant project, three organizations are critical to your research:

1. Foundation Center (http://foundationcenter.org)
2. Council on Foundations (www.cof.org)
3. The Grantsmanship Center (www.tgci.com)

Foundation Center

The Foundation Center (http://foundationcenter.org; see figure 5.11) is the largest producer of directories and databases of grant-giving foundations. Its goal is to connect nonprofits to grant makers. They have many resources for researching foundations, discovering trends in grant making, and finding top foundations in your geographic region. The Foundation Center's website provides many tools (see the following list), including an Online Librarian available via chat or e-mail, resource centers, print resources, online databases, and a resource for finding foundation stats.

- The *Foundation Directory Online* (*FDO*) (http://foundationcenter.org/products/ foundation-directory-online) is an online subscription database that includes more than 140,000 funders and is updated weekly. It also includes a prospect management platform. Using the online database allows you to search multiple fields simultaneously, provides in-depth information about the funders and their grants, and includes links to funder websites and annual reports. There are different subscription plans, including a monthly option.
- The *Foundation Directory Online* Quick Start (http://foundationcenter.org/ find-funding/fdo-quick-start) is a free search tool that provides public access to essential information about more than 100,000 foundations and over 250,000 IRS Forms 990-PF (Private Foundation).
- The Foundation Center operates five regional library/learning centers nationwide and more than 470 Funding Information Networks (formerly called Cooperating

FIGURE 5.11

FOUNDATION CENTER WEBSITE

Collections) in all fifty states and Puerto Rico. Use the center's GrantSpace Find Us search (http://grantspace.org/find-us) to locate a resource center in your area. These free funding information centers focus on private funding sources and are located in libraries or nonprofit information centers. Many Funding Information Networks include access to the *Foundation Directory Online* (see earlier entry, normally a fee-based subscription service) in addition to numerous print directories.

- The Foundation Center's Foundation Stats (http://data.foundationcenter.org) provides a comprehensive resource for accessing data and generating tables and charts on the size, scope, and giving priorities of the U.S. foundation community.

- GrantSpace (http://grantspace.org), a free service of the Foundation Center, includes access to webinars, podcasts, reference assistance, training, resources for grants, and more.

Once you identify possible funders, you can narrow your search by referring to the *Foundation Directory Online* Quick Start for more information about a particular foundation. Using this free database, you can access detailed information, including background, program areas, fields of interest, and financial data, such as 990s. This free resource can be easier to navigate than a foundation's site, and the Foundation Center claims that nearly 90 percent of foundations don't have a website.

The Council on Foundations

The Council on Foundations (www.cof.org) provides information about research, publications, conferences, and workshops. It offers links to community foundations, corporate foundations and giving programs, family and public foundations, and international grant makers. The mission of the organization is "to provide the opportunity, leadership and tools needed by philanthropic organizations to expand, enhance and sustain their ability to advance the common good."

The Grantsmanship Center

The Grantsmanship Center (www.tgci.com) maintains information about your state's foundations, community foundations, corporate giving programs, and the top forty foundations that give in your state. Visit the center's "Funding State by State" page (www.tgci.com/funding-sources).

Community Foundation Resources

Over 700 community foundations serve specific geographic areas and often have solid collections of materials about writing proposals as well as print, electronic, and local directories of funding sources. They may also offer classes for community members about their funding and resources. Visit your local community foundation to use its library or collection of information on local corporations and foundations to access extensive information about local corporations and foundations that you may not find collected in any other place. Tell your community foundation about your project idea and ask about appropriate funding sources. Its goal is to match funders with organizations like yours, so establish a relationship and check in with the foundation periodically. The foundation's website may also list grant opportunity announcements and application guidelines.

You can find your local community foundation using the Community Foundation Locator from the Council on Foundations (www.cof.org/community-foundation-locator; see figure 5.12).

FIGURE 5.12

COMMUNITY FOUNDATION LOCATOR

Corporate Grant Resources

Many major corporations and businesses have created foundations or giving programs with funds generated from their profits. Some companies operate an in-house corporate giving program in addition to a foundation. Local businesses often want to give back to their communities, and corporations want to demonstrate their civic responsibility.

In general, corporations give to organizations in the communities in which they operate. Visit the websites and offices of the businesses and corporations that operate in your community for information about their priorities, grant guidelines, and deadlines. On their websites you may see a link to "community," "community giving," "community involvement," or "community relations." Corporations operating in your area may have community giving programs or may offer other donations, such as supplies or equipment, to support your needs. Visit websites of corporations that operate in your community for information about their priorities, grant guidelines, and deadlines. Target, Dollar General, Best Buy, Walmart, and Barnes & Noble all have giving programs. Dollar General is an example of a corporate foundation with several national giving opportunities applicable to libraries (see, e.g., figure 5.13).

Many corporations devote entire sections of their websites to explaining what they fund in their communities and how to apply. You may even find an online application that you can submit electronically. Each corporate site is arranged differently, so you may need to explore a little to get to the information you need. If you have questions, contact the corporation's community outreach office. Personnel there are usually happy to talk to you about what they fund and where to find additional information.

FIGURE 5.13

DOLLAR GENERAL LITERACY FOUNDATION WEBSITE

The following are some notable resources for finding corporate funders:

- *Corporate Giving Directory: Comprehensive Profiles of America's Major Corporate Foundations and Corporate Giving Programs* provides complete profiles of the 1,000 largest corporate foundations and corporate direct-giving programs in the United States, representing nearly $5.6 billion in cash and nonmonetary support annually. The directory is available from Information Today (books.infotoday.com/directories/CorporateGivingDirectory.shtml).
- *National Directory of Corporate Giving*, published by the Foundation Center, includes detailed portraits of over 4,000 companies and corporate foundations and over 1,700 direct corporate giving programs. Included are application guidelines, key personnel, types of support awarded, giving limitations, and financial data, including assets, annual giving, and the average size of grants.
- *Foundation Directory Online* is an online database that includes information on over 4,000 corporate donors that support nonprofit organizations and programs. There is a free version that can be used to search grant makers and 990s (https://fdo.foundationcenter.org).
- *Corporate Philanthropy Report* includes corporate grant information, funding opportunities, and insight into who's funding what, including contact names and phone numbers. It also provides advice on how to take advantage of corporate giving opportunities. This report is available from Jossey-Bass, a division of John Wiley & Sons (www.corporatephilanthropyreport.com).
- The Grantsmanship Center's "Funding State-by-State" offers information on corporate giving. First, click on your state, and then you can select "Corporate Giving Programs in [your state]" (www.tgci.com/funding-sources).

Club and Organization Resources

Clubs and organizations may have a service, civic, or skills-based focus. Organizations such as the Lions Club, Rotary, the Association of Junior Leagues, and Kiwanis usually have local chapters. These organizations often have giving programs that involve smaller gifts focused on supporting their individual communities through service, materials, and financial investments.

Your local *Yellow Pages*, library board or Friends group, and staff members may also help identify clubs and organizations that provide funding.

Professional and Trade Association Resources

Professional associations often make grant funds available to their members. Grants and awards are available for library organizations and individuals. Grants may be offered to support the planning and implementation of programs, to aid in the preparation of a dissertation or other publications, and to promote research in library and information sciences. Grants are also given to support continuing education opportunities, such as travel to conferences or other events that can broaden an individual's experience or education in librarianship.

Hundreds of grants, awards, and scholarships are available from the American Library Association, Public Library Association, regional library associations, and others. For more information, visit the following webpages:

- "PLA Awards and Grants" (www.ala.org/pla/awards)
- ALA's "Awards, Grants and Scholarships" (www.ala.org/awardsgrants)
- ALA's "State and Regional Chapters" (www.ala.org/groups/affiliates/chapters/state/stateregional)

Staying Aware of New Grant Opportunities

An important part of your research is staying up-to-date with new grant opportunities. Subscribe to some free resources, such as these blogs, e-mail notification services, and electronic newsletters:

- Michigan State University Libraries' "Nonprofit Funding Newsletters and Current Awareness Services" (http://staff.lib.msu.edu/harris23/grants/percat2.htm#rfpbulletin) provides a list of valuable resources.
- The *Library Grants* blog (http://librarygrants.blogspot.com), a free service we have offered since 2005, is a shortcut to finding library grants. We post new grants every month, and at times every week. For each grant, we include the deadline, a brief description, and a link to more information. To save you time in grant seeking, we verify with every grant opportunity that libraries of some type are eligible to apply, we include only national or large regional grants, and we remove the listings once the deadlines have passed. All types of grants are posted. Visit our blog and subscribe to the RSS feed.
- *Philanthropy News Digest* and *RFP Bulletin* provide a weekly roundup of recently announced RFPs from private, corporate, and government funding sources. Each RFP listing provides a brief overview of the funding opportunity as well as a link to the complete RFP. Subscribe to this and other electronic

newsletters at the Foundation Center website (http://foundationcenter.org/newsletters).

- Grants.gov offers several ways to receive notifications of new grant opportunity postings and updates by subscribing to the following e-mail notification services or RSS feeds (www.grants.gov/web/grants/manage-subscriptions.html):

  - The "Subscribe to a specific grant opportunity" option allows you to receive grant announcement notifications based on federally assigned, unique FONs.
  - "Subscribe to saved searches for grant opportunities" triggers e-mail notifications about grant opportunities related to specific search criteria, such as funding instrument type, eligibility, and subagency.
  - The "Subscribe to new grant opportunities" option will get you a daily e-mail list of all new grants.
  - You can also subscribe to Grants.gov RSS feeds for new or modified opportunities by agency or category.

- On IMLS's "E-mail Subscriptions" page (www.imls.gov/news-events/e-mail-subscriptions), you can subscribe to IMLS newsletters, grant announcements, and areas of interest.
- On *The Chronicle of Philanthropy*'s "Get Free Email Subscriptions" page (philanthropy.com/page/Get-Newsletters/543?cid=cpf_nwsl) you can subscribe to the *Philanthropy Today* free e-mail newsletter and other alerts.
- If you are at an academic institution, investigate grant alert opportunities through your grants and contracts or research office. Subscription databases may include GrantForward, InfoEd SPIN, GrantSelect, GrantsWire, or Grant Advisor Plus.

Talking with Funders

As you wrap up your research, you can contact funders to clarify your questions and discuss their possible interest in your project. Remember that funders are people, not ATMs, and grant work involves building relationships with them. At this point in your research, you should feel comfortable calling any of the contacts on your "match" list should questions or concerns arise. Before you start writing a grant proposal, you should be very sure that you understand the criteria and that the funder would be interested in your project. Don't be hesitant about contacting potential grant funders. Once you've reviewed the grant proposal and other materials, if you have questions or just want to make sure your grant project is one they will be interested in funding, send them an e-mail or ask for a quick phone conversation. If your project is not a match with a particular funder, ask if that funder knows of other potential funders who would be a better match. It is much better to check in and make sure your project will match a funder's interests before you go through the process of writing and submitting a proposal.

◇◇◇◇◇◇◇◇◇◇◇◇◇◇◇◇◇

The last two chapters have been all about grant matchmaking, finding the right governmental, foundation, corporate, or organizational funder whose priorities are in alignment with your library and the specific grant that fits with your project. In part III (see p. 184) and online (www.alaeditions.org/webextras), you'll find a handout on funding sources and resources, Winning Grants Sources and Resources Handout, and a Funder Summary Worksheet for documenting your research.

Some other things you can do to find the right funder:

- Read publications like newsletters, journals, and local newspapers for funding opportunities.
- Subscribe to the *Library Grants* blog (http://librarygrants.blogspot.com).
- Subscribe to other grant-related RSS feeds and electronic discussion groups.
- Contact other libraries in your area that have received grants.
- Talk with potential funders about their interests and priorities.

Creating and Submitting the Winning Proposal

Writing the winning proposal requires planning and organization. It is very important to realize that the beginning of the grant process doesn't start with a grant application. All the planning and organizing completed in previous steps help this part of the grant process flow smoothly. Having a strategic plan as the foundation of your grant work ensures you are supporting your library's mission and goals and the needs of your community. This demonstrates to funders that the grant project is well planned and truly needed, not just a random idea.

Make certain you have met any necessary stipulations dictated by your library's infrastructure, whether that means your city, school, or university policies on grant work. You also must be aware of any local procedures or requirements that would affect your library's ability to apply for the grant opportunity you've selected.

Putting together an effective grant proposal is more than just answering questions and filling out forms. You must have accurately examined your community, the current issues, and the societal impacts affecting the people you serve. Just because you admire the library programs in a nearby town does not mean they would be a good fit for your community. You should understand the grant maker you are approaching, as your grant project should support not just your library's mission but also your community's and the funder's interests, priorities, needs, and wants.

Begin by carefully reading the entire grant application, especially the qualifications, deadlines, and evaluation criteria. You don't want to be almost finished writing a proposal when you realize that you do not qualify, you've missed a deadline, you needed to partner with the local health department, or you must provide unplanned services. Highlight any questions you have and make a list of the resources and materials you will need. Underline key words or phrases you might want to incorporate into your proposal. The Grant Submission Checklist (see figure 6.2 at the end of this chapter) can be helpful for organizing this information. It is also provided in part III (see p. 195) and online (www.ala editions.org/webextras) so you can adapt it to your specific needs.

Be prepared to write one or more drafts until your proposal is concise and easily understood. You don't want to have a grant rejected due to just typographical errors. Let others read your proposal and get their feedback. Especially helpful are those who are not connected to the library or the project. Even a family

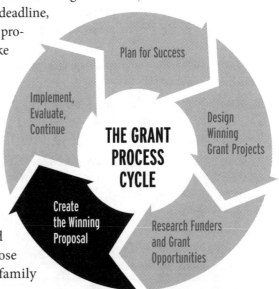

THE GRANT PROCESS CYCLE

Plan for Success

Design Winning Grant Projects

Research Funders and Grant Opportunities

Create the Winning Proposal

Implement, Evaluate, Continue

ACTIVE VERBS

- achieve
- analyze
- assess
- assist
- change
- conclude
- connect
- coordinate
- create
- decide
- define
- demonstrate
- design
- develop
- direct
- educate
- elevate
- engage
- ensure
- establish
- evaluate
- identify
- illuminate
- illustrate
- implement
- indicate
- inform
- inspire
- instruct
- investigate
- involve
- lead
- learn
- maintain
- manage
- motivate
- organize
- plan
- prepare
- promote
- provide
- validate

member could provide an interesting and helpful perspective. Just ask others to read your proposal for fifteen minutes and then tell you what they understood. Why fifteen minutes? This may be more time than most preliminary reviewers will give your proposal on the first read-through. Objective readers can also catch any use of library lingo or acronyms that might be confusing to a grant reviewer. If they didn't immediately see what you want to achieve, rewrite it until it is clear. We've reviewed some grant proposals in which we were unable to discern exactly what the library was looking to fund. It should not be difficult to understand exactly how much you are requesting or for what purpose.

Writing Tips

Writing a proposal is different from other types of writing. Proposal writing is similar to sales or marketing work, or even good storytelling. You are attempting to convince the funder to sponsor and support your idea and project. Your proposal should tell the story of the people in your community, the need that they have, and how your project—supported by the funder's grant—can make a positive and even life-changing impact in their lives. You want the funder to see real people with real problems. Your well-planned grant project is the resolution to their need. You are probably very passionate about your grant project, so make sure you convey that enthusiasm in your grant proposal. Unless you are dealing with a seriously bureaucratic grant maker, don't be afraid to appeal to the grant reviewer's emotions, as long as you balance your assertions with valid data.

Making your story come alive is especially important in the proposal summary or abstract, as some grant reviewers may use only this *one* section of your grant to judge your entire proposal. At the very least, your summary or abstract will make a first impression that will color the reviewer's approach to the rest of your proposal.

Display confidence and capability by approaching your project with the belief that it will be successful. Use language throughout your proposal that shows positive assurance. Demonstrate your ability to achieve the outcomes you've set. Your grant proposal must show that you will be able to implement the project with success. Be persuasive, and reinforce your claims with plans, as bravado alone will not impress a funder. Include facts, research, and specific plans with your goals, measurable objectives, and outcomes.

Proposals should also be concise. Elaborations should add depth and scope, insight, and interest. The proposal will be judged on content, not weight.

For a powerful and energetic proposal, avoid using passive verbs, such as *was* and *were*, or static verbs, such as *am, is, are, be, have, do, could, should*, and *would*. Use active verbs instead.

Using the active voice and including details on how you are preparing to implement the grant will demonstrate that you own the project and the work it will involve. For instance, "Library staff will collaborate with a local community college curriculum development advisor to create and provide technology classes especially designed for older adults based on topics determined in the needs assessment" communicates a much different sense of your relationship to the project than does "Technology classes will be provided."

Collaborating within Your Organization

Grants.gov Workspace is a relatively new option for individuals or organizations applying for funding opportunities. Workspace is a shared, online environment where members of the same organization may simultaneously access and edit different forms within an application. For each funding opportunity announcement (FOA), you can create individual workspaces. Find out more at the Grants.gov "Workspace Overview" page (www.grants.gov/web/grants/applicants/workspace -overview.html).

There are free services, such as Dropbox and Google Docs, that you can use for sharing basic information and working on documents together. You can also use project management software, such as Basecamp (https://basecamp.com), to assign tasks, track deadlines, and facilitate online discussions. See more about project management software in chapter 7.

Role of Partners and Collaborators

Whether required or not, show any collaboration and partnerships in your proposal. Partners can help with sustainability and ensure community support. Collaborations are also a beneficial way to share equipment, expertise, and resources and produce a wider impact. Letters of commitment, memoranda of understanding (MOUs), and partnership agreements help document a partnership and designate responsibilities. A sample partnership agreement is included in part III (see p. 168) and online (www .alaeditions.org/webextras), and it can be a great addition to your grant proposal.

Emphasize collaboration and partnerships throughout your proposal. Some funders are now requiring partnerships and/or collaborations. Ignoring a partnership requirement can cost you a grant win. You can often have a wider impact when more organizations are involved. You should be contacting other community organizations as part of your library outreach, so finding collaborators shouldn't be difficult. These relationships should be ongoing and not just limited to grant work. Your library should have representatives at community meetings (chamber of commerce, Lions Club, Kiwanis, etc.), planning or task force discussions, and so forth. Even if partners are not required, funders will admire that you are planning for sustainability and ensuring future community support.

Nonprofits often are pleased to partner with libraries if there are similar goals. Partnerships between libraries, schools, colleges, museums, religious groups, and community organizations are often successful as well. For example, if you want to assist your community with unemployment issues, find valuable partners that provide job training, child care, GED preparation, or other social services to create a program with many ways to benefit and support job seekers.

Communicating with Funders

If you have questions that aren't answered in the application or want to discuss potential grant project ideas, call the funder or set up a time to meet with a local funder. The funder will then be familiar with your project and library when you submit a proposal.

Don't be apprehensive about contacting the funder if you have questions that aren't answered in the RFP or application materials. Most charitable organizations have been created out of a desire to be part of the solution to societal problems. The reason they extend grants is to help fulfill their own missions. Funders give money to meet their goals; it is their job, and they are there to help. Of course, be certain you've done your research first and that you're not asking a question already answered in the funder's documentation. You don't want to bother a funder and become a nuisance, but if you call with a realistic inquiry, it should be welcomed. An added benefit is that the funder will be familiar with your proposal before it has been submitted. This is a good way to start building a communicative partnership with the funder. Building trust and identifying mutual goals are essential to successful grant work. You may even want to set up a time to meet in person with local funders to start building good relationships. Figure 6.1 provides a Questions for Funders Checklist (also included in part III on p. 187 and online at www .alaeditions.org/webextras) that includes questions you may want to ask.

FIGURE 6.1

QUESTIONS FOR FUNDERS CHECKLIST

- ☐ Is my library eligible for your grants?
- ☐ How are applications reviewed?
- ☐ Are specific screening criteria or a rubric used? May we have a copy?
- ☐ May we submit a draft of the grant proposal for review before the final deadline?
- ☐ If I briefly describe the project, would you provide suggestions or advice?
- ☐ Are copies of successful grant proposals available?
- ☐ May we include our strategic plan or other supporting documentation in an appendix?
- ☐ May we include a table of contents?
- ☐ How and when are final decisions made?
- ☐ Will we be notified that our grant proposal has been received?

Applying to Multiple Funders

You may want to apply to more than one funder at a time. If you are submitting proposals to several different funders, you should indicate this in the proposal. For example, you might state, "In addition to your foundation, this proposal is being submitted to the Community Foundation and the Mr. Wealthy Benefactor Foundation" or "We have already received a grant of $30,000 from the Happy to Give Foundation and are requesting $15,000 from your organization, which is the balance required for the project." This will not be viewed negatively, as funders often view multiple funding sources as a significant factor in the sustainability of projects. However, if you use the same grant proposal, make sure you customize it for each funder. Some funders have told us that they have received proposals with another agency's name on them—not a very good first impression for your proposal!

Application Review Process

Funders evaluate proposals in different ways. Some funders send proposals to reviewers who rate them based on a predetermined scoring system. Other systems for evaluating proposals may include review committees or panels of government officials, experts in a specific field, community-based reviewers, or a multiphase process. Some funders distribute the individual sections of the proposal to different reviewers. For example, one reviewer may be focused on judging the specific project you are proposing, while a different reviewer will focus on examining the evaluation process you have specified or the budget. Some funders use external proposal reviewers on a contract basis or as volunteers. These reviewers may be subject specialists, and they may be reading hundreds of grants.

The funder's proposal evaluation method is usually outlined in the grant guidelines; however, if it is not, you can find out this information by contacting the funding agency. Make sure you know the funder's timeline so you will have an idea about when you will hear whether or not your project has been funded.

Many grants are very competitive, which means that reviewers have numerous proposals to read and a lot of hard decisions to make. Ensuring that your proposal is clear and easy to comprehend will increase your chances of success. As with any type of writing, it is important to keep your audience in mind—those who read, review, and make decisions about your proposal. More than one person will probably be evaluating your proposal. It may be a committee that reviews your proposal, with each individual reviewer scoring your proposal on established criteria. Make it easy for the grant reviewer to find the information requested by following the same format and headings as the application. Never assume any specific knowledge on the part of the reader. Do not assume that the reader will know that libraries are doing incredible work or that you are informed of your community's needs, and don't assume that the reader will know the duties of a reference librarian or the programming and supplies involved for a summer reading program.

Being a grant reviewer is not easy work. Difficult decisions must be made. We have given grant workshops in which we use an exercise that involves our participants forming review committees. The groups are given grant proposals and must quickly decide how to distribute funding. We are always amazed at how passionate people become, defending their choices and arguing for one grant proposal over another. We remind them that this is pretend money and these are pretend organizations, but it is an amazing demonstration of how some decisions are personally biased. You may assume that it will be clear which proposals stand out and should be funded, but some decisions are arbitrary. It isn't as easy to "give money away" as one may think, and often there are heated debates and compromises made, such as giving less funding to one organization so that another grant can be funded as well. This is another reason why it can be helpful to build relationships with funders and get early feedback as to what they are looking for and how your library can best present your case.

Decisions to give (like most human decisions) are emotional. Facts by themselves are not persuasive and do not motivate people to give. Provide fact-based, verifiable statements, of course, but include the passion you feel for the community you serve. Remember that you are communicating with decision makers who are real people. If the funder is a good match, you share values and you can show how your project can help fulfill that funder's goals.

Specifications and Requirements

The content of the proposal should be tailored to any specifications found in the grant guidelines. This may include such details as the number of pages allowed, required forms, formatting particulars, and number of copies. Each detail is important. If a funder receives thousands of grants, it is easy to whittle down the number of applicants by rejecting those who do not comply with instructions. For example, some funders specify that proposals should not be bound, as they may need to make copies for multiple reviewers. So before you spend the extra time and funds to produce a beautifully packaged manuscript, be sure you are fulfilling the funder's specified requests. We know of a case where a federal agency rejected a grant application without reading it because part of the proposal was not double-spaced, as specified in the guidelines.

Match the arrangement of the sections in the grant proposal to that used in the application; don't change the order of the sections even if it makes more sense to you to do so. Match the names of the section headings in your proposal to the section headings provided in the instructions. This will allow the reviewer to easily determine that all required information is included. Reviewers should never have to search for needed information. The proposal should be neat, organized, and professional. Make a checklist of the specifications so that you can ensure that you've met them. For an example, see the Grant Submission Checklist in figure 6.2 at the end of this chapter.

Types of Applications

There are three types of applications: letters of intent or inquiry, RFPs, and online proposals. Let's look at each in more detail.

Letter of Intent or Inquiry Letter

Funders may ask for a letter of intent so that they can quickly decide whether yours is a project that they would like to fund. If the funder accepts your letter of intent, then you may be asked to submit a longer, more detailed proposal. The letter of intent is usually a two- to three-page summary that gives a brief description of the project, the amount requested, the need, and a brief organizational overview. This letter should focus on how the project aligns with the funder's mission and goals. It should describe the needs and then outline the project. Write succinctly and clearly, organizing your case so that the funder can quickly make a decision.

Similarly, you might contact a funder with an inquiry letter. Using the same type of information as you would include in a letter of intent, you would send this letter if you were considering applying for a grant from a funder but were unsure if your library or project fits the funder's scope of work.

Request for Proposal or Grant Application

This is the typical grant proposal and is sometimes called a request for proposal or a grant application. Several examples can be accessed by following the links on our *Library Grants* blog (http://librarygrants.blogspot.com). Some funders provide lengthy forms, while others give brief guidelines or have an online application process. Funders will have differing priorities, deadlines, and approaches to the funding process. The good news is that although there are differences, most funders are essentially asking for the same information. They just may use different wording or prefer a different order. This means that once you've gone through the Grant Process Cycle and written one quality grant proposal, the subsequent proposals will be less challenging and will not require the same intensive background work as the first. Common application forms are shared by some organizations, usually in a specific geographic area. Some grant applications require only a brief one-page form, while others might be thirty to forty pages, and some federal government applications may be hundreds of pages long.

Online Proposal

Many funders, especially government organizations, require proposals to be submitted online. The websites usually provide detailed instructions with FAQs and contact information for questions related to electronic submissions. Some websites have forms that you can download to your computer, fill out, and then upload to submit. Others have an electronic form that must be completed while connected to the Internet. First, create the proposal in a word processor, and then you can easily cut and paste into the online form. Always make sure you have a backup copy and try to submit as early as possible, as servers do get overloaded on the last submission day if too many applicants submit at one time, which may cause you to miss the deadline.

Key Grant Proposal Components

The content of the proposal should be tailored to specifications in the grant guidelines, including details such as the number of pages, required forms, formatting particulars, and number of copies. As noted earlier, if a funder receives thousands of grants, it is easy to reduce the number of applicants by rejecting those who do not comply with instructions. Try to match the arrangement and names of the sections of the grant proposal to those in the application, so that the reviewer can easily find all required information without having to search. Make sure each section can be comprehended independently.

There are many ways to organize proposals. The RFP will stipulate the requirements, and some are more detailed than others. Read the guidelines for specifications about required information and how it should be arranged. Most grant proposals are usually fifteen or fewer pages. Government grants may require that you fill out lengthy forms and may be a lot longer. The Grant Proposal Worksheet, provided in part III (see p. 188) and online (www.alaeditions.org/webextras), is an example of a typical grant application that includes all the common components that you can customize to create your own application. The following are the most standard grant proposal components:

- Title sheet
- Cover letter
- Table of contents
- Proposal summary or abstract
- Organizational overview
- Statement of needs

- Project description
- Timeline
- Budget
- Evaluation process
- Appendix

If you have been following our Grant Process Cycle, you should have compiled most of the information needed during the project planning phase covered in chapter 2.

Title Sheet

This is your opportunity to display creativity and develop an ingenious title for your project or program—something that the grant reviewer will remember. However, if you are not particularly inspired, don't let this be a stumbling block. A title that is descriptive and informative is perfectly acceptable. You should also include the name of the funding organization, the name and address of the submitting library, and the date.

Cover Letter

This basic letter outlines your proposal and sets the tone. It should be easy to read, interesting, convincing, and comprehensive. Anyone reading this cover letter should be able to quickly determine exactly what your organization does, the purpose or reason for your request, and the amount of the request.

Keep it to one page and use your library's or organization's letterhead. The header should include the date, the name of the contact person at the funding organization, the name and address of the funding organization, and the title of your grant. The first paragraph should declare your pleasure in submitting the grant in order to serve your target audience. Include a few sentences that describe your project, including outcomes, needs, target audience, why your library is a good match, grant partners, the amount of funding requested, any in-kind or matching or outside grant funds, and any major planning accomplished. Conclude by offering to provide additional information and have the library director or another authority sign.

Incorporate the following information from your Project Planning Worksheet:

- Grant project title
- A few sentences from your project description, including outcomes
- Needs statement
- Two to three sentences from your organizational overview
- Names of grant project partners
- Funding requested and any in-kind, matching, or outside grant funds
- Any planning accomplished and involvement of the target audience

Conclude the letter with an offer to provide additional information if any is needed. The library director or another authority should sign the cover letter.

Table of Contents

As in a book, a table of contents will help organize your proposal and make it easy for reviewers to locate necessary information. Different reviewers may be responsible for analyzing different parts of your proposal, so make sure each section can be comprehended independently. If it is not specified in the guidelines that you should include a table of contents, this may be one of the questions you want to ask the funder.

Proposal Summary or Abstract

The most important part of your grant proposal is the proposal abstract or summary because it serves as the first impression and can be critical to the success of the proposal. It may be carefully scrutinized to determine if the rest of the proposal should even be considered, so it needs to be able to stand on its own. Even though it is often the first section of a proposal, it should be written last to make sure it contains all elements of your grant proposal. You should be succinct, sell your idea, and make your point precisely. You should present your whole case: what you want to do, why it's important, why you will succeed, and how much it will cost. It should be immediately clear why your project is unique and so compelling that the funder will want to immediately read your entire proposal. Be sure to avoid any library jargon that may be unclear or unfamiliar to the reviewer. This abstract should tie in to the funder's mission and display the project's impact and how the project will help fulfill the funder's goals.

The summary will essentially be a condensed form of your entire proposal. Nothing should be in your summary that is not in your proposal. Include the following in your summary:

- Library's exact legal name and full mailing address
- Contact information for the library director and the grant coordinator
- A few sentences summarizing the library's organizational overview, showing why the library is the best choice for implementing the grant project
- Project title

- Project description (from your Project Planning Worksheet), including the needs statement and the target audience, and a summary of the project goals
- Partners
- Amount requested, including project funding from other sources
- Project time period
- Brief overview of the evaluation methods to be used

Organizational Overview

Before funders will invest in a program, they must be certain that the funding will be managed by a capable, dependable, effective organization. The overview helps the funder judge the integrity and worthiness of your library. This is your opportunity to sell what it is you do. Libraries have an instant reputation of credibility and trust, but remember that not everyone understands everything a library does, so don't assume that funders will understand library terminology or basic processes. Libraries are the centers of communities, but to some people, they only represent books.

In chapter 2, we discussed library and community profiles, which may be what is needed for this section. Academic and special libraries may also need to include broader information on their entire organizations. Usually, funders will want to know your library's history and mission, whom you serve, achievements, primary programs, current budget, leadership, board members, and key staff members. Brief success and human interest stories can be included, but these should be relevant to the project and to the specific funder's interests. Answer these questions: "Who are we?" "How are we qualified?" "Why should we be trusted?" A funder needs to deem your organization trustworthy and reliant for a true partnership to develop. Having a strategic plan is another way to demonstrate that your organization is well managed. If an appendix of supporting material is allowed, including the library's strategic plan can be beneficial.

Granting agencies want to make the best use of their funding, and they want to be assured that your project will be successful and help fulfill both your mission and theirs. If you've done your research, your organization should be a good match with the funders you choose, so as they are reading your overview, they should immediately recognize similarities in mission, vision, and goals. A great match will mean that reviewers think to themselves, "Hey, we want to accomplish the same things!"

Statement of Needs

In this section, you will describe the current situation in your community and how your project will address it. Chapter 2 discusses how to conduct a community needs assessment, to show what your community really does require, and how to develop library and community profiles. If you have completed these profiles, they will be very helpful for writing this section of your grant proposal.

Provide a compelling, logical reason why the proposal should be supported and is important. Start with the facts and then move on to the solution. This is not a list of wants; it is an explanation of the need that your project is designed to meet by bringing about a change in your target audience. Support this assessment by including qualified research and evidence to justify the need. Use both statistics and human interest stories for supporting examples. Include data that is historical, geographic, quantitative, and factual. Identify any other existing projects being implemented in your library or community that are related to the problem.

Remember that the need is never for things—not for new computers, new chairs, new books—but for solving a problem or addressing a need in your community. Focus on how the library can help improve your community. Funders want to help people, not buy things. Your proposal should tell the story of the people who will be helped.

Avoid describing the needs of your library as the problem. Not having enough computers at your library is not the problem. Rather, the problem might be the increase in deaths due to preventable illness and lack of health literacy. Providing more consumer health materials and health-related programming on free online health databases is a better solution. Explain how you will attempt to fulfill the need. Define what you intend to do.

For example, one rural librarian wanted to apply for books for the children in her community. She filled out a Project Planning Worksheet, and we reviewed it for her. When describing the need in her community that the project would address, she wrote, "Kids will have books." In the goals section, she wrote, "Get books for kids." In the section addressing changes to the community and action steps to take, she wrote, "Get books for kids." When we sat down to discuss her grant project, she said, "I can think up great ideas for grants, but when it is time to sit down and write about them, I get a mental block." So we asked her *why* she wanted the children to have books. She described her situation very enthusiastically: "Oh! We live in a very rural, very poor town. Many of the children don't own a single book of their own. I want to get a grant so we can give them a book of their own. One they can write their name in, take home with them, and read again and again. A book they can select based on their interests and that they can take pride in starting their own book collection and enjoying reading books from the library as well. I want them to not have to worry about the date it is due, and to have a brand new book of their own." Of course, this is a much more compelling need argument than just "Kids need books." We wanted to go and buy those kids some books right then! She was passionate about her project and about wanting to help the children. Her community had a real need, and many funders are interested in giving books to rural libraries. She just needed to figure out how to be as compelling in her writing as she was in person. When writing your grant proposal, don't forget that real people with real feelings will be reviewing it. Don't be afraid to appeal to their emotive interests.

Sometimes it is all about the phrasing. For example, your library has experienced budget cuts and you have had to cut staff. There are long checkout lines and your board thinks you could convert to using RFID (radio frequency identification) technology so you can install self-checkout. Of course, this is not in your budget, so the board tells you to write a grant. When writing this proposal, it is important to think about what the real benefits are for the community. *Not*: The lines are too long and we can't afford desk staff. *Instead*: Focus on how RFID will free staff from checking out books so they can be available for community programs and one-on-one assistance, and on how patrons will be able to check out books faster, with shorter lines. Explain how RFID technology will benefit those using your library.

Don't put the focus on the state's or the country's needs, unless your project will serve those larger regions, but rather focus on the needs of your specific and unique community. The exact target population should be identified. Many funders are interested in knowing that the people who will benefit from the project are actually supportive of the grant. If the audience has had input and has assisted with designing the program, make sure you include this information. Projects that are created with the involvement and input of the targeted population are more likely to be successful.

Prove why the library has the ability to respond to the need you have identified. Link the fulfillment of the need to your library's mission. Answer the questions:

- Why this issue?
- Why this target population?
- Why this funder?
- Why your library?

Use data to support your arguments. Include qualified research and evidence to justify the need, using both statistics and human interest stories. Connect the fulfillment of the need to your library's mission. Use the following links to find useful statistics to prove need in your grant proposal and to research the community members of your target population:

- *U.S. Census Bureau, American FactFinder* (factfinder2.census.gov/faces/nav/jsf/pages/index.xhtml): This is an excellent source for U.S. population, housing, economic, and geographic data. Statistical profiles of communities are based on several censuses and surveys. American FactFinder is a fundamental source of information to identify or confirm the education, health, economic, or other needs of individuals, families, and communities.
- *IMLS, Surveys & Data* (www.imls.gov/research-tools/data-collection): IMLS collects data through several surveys and provides several tools for assessing the data that can be helpful for grant work. Surveys include the Public Libraries Survey, the State Library Administrative Agency Survey, and the Public Needs for Libraries and Museum Services Survey.
- IMLS, "*Data Catalog*" (data.imls.gov): In 2015, IMLS launched an open data catalog site which includes IMLS data about grants administration, museums, libraries, and related organizations.
- *ALA, "Research and Statistics Resources"* (www.ala.org/research): This page offers a list of numerous library statistics sites.
- *Public Libraries, "State Libraries"* (www.publiclibraries.com/state_library.htm): Here you can click on your state library agency to access statistics about libraries in your state.
- *USA.gov, "Data and Statistics about the United States"* (www.usa.gov/statistics): Find data about the United States, such as demographic, economic, and health information.

Project Description

This section is a more in-depth narrative than the project summary. In the latter section, you discussed the needs, and now you will focus on the solutions. Acknowledge that you are aware of several solutions and that you have chosen the approach that will be most successful. State the advantages and any limitations of the solutions.

You should explain the significance of your project. Clarify how your work differs from, is related to, or extends earlier work. Back this up with research. Funders are more inclined toward a well-thought-out project that includes assurances of sustainability and appropriate use of funds. Funders want to fund projects that will be successful, and these are often the indicators.

Don't assume that the reader is familiar with the subject. You could include articles in the appendix to support topics with which they may be unfamiliar. For example, if requesting a computer lab, you could include studies done on public access computing, the digital divide, and the number of people who use library computers. This is an especially important part of your grant application to have someone outside of your organization review to ensure that it is easy to comprehend.

Include information on your target population, specifically, the number to be served, how you will attract them to the project, and how you will involve them. You can have more than one target population, for example, a reading program that involves children and their parents.

Sustainability of projects can be a big obstacle. Funders realize this and are more likely to favor organizations that address this issue in their proposals. Having partners and supporters and showing that you are investigating other sources of funding for the future, including matching funds, will help prove your project isn't short term, but instead one that is worth investing in and supporting because it will make a true difference. Also include any ways that the project might leverage impact for other library goals or for other community needs.

Demonstrate that you have done your research and planning. This will enable the funder to see that you are prepared and committed to implementing the project. Some funders would rather support new activities and programs rather than existing ones. They would like to be connected to something original, exciting, and groundbreaking. They want to see that their funding will make a difference that wouldn't otherwise be possible. Try to show how your project could support these desires.

Include the following topics and information:

- Project significance and uniqueness (include one or two sentences developed from the needs statement)
- Target audience
- Project goals
- Project objectives
- Project partners
- Plans for sustainability and leveraging impact

Timeline

This section can require a lot of detail. In chapter 3, you identified project activities from your goals and objectives. These activities will define how you are going to accomplish your project goals. In your timeline, you will estimate the duration of each major activity of your project—from the moment you get the grant check until the conclusion of your grant project when you are evaluating its success. This may be portrayed through a calendar format with start and end dates, project activities, and outcomes listed. If you are unsure of specific dates, you can instead break the timeline into months; for example, Months 1–2: Recruit and hire temporary employees; Months 3–4: Form advisory committees and publish website. See chapter 3 for a sample timeline.

Budget

Budgets are cost projections and should be very detailed and well researched. Some funders will provide budget forms that must be submitted with the proposal, while others are less specific. See chapter 3 for more details about budget planning. The application may include a budget request section that covers the grant project specifically and another area to include the entire organizational budget. Costs should be reasonable and accompanied by thorough explanations. Although it may be difficult to calculate some of the necessities, make a good effort. Taking the time to obtain exact costs instead of estimating will not only keep your budget detailed but also ensure that you really have enough funds to cover what you want to do. You most likely will want to involve your fiscal office or financial administrators at this point, as they may have a better awareness of cost projections and your library budget. Incorrect budget balancing is one of the most common errors in grant proposals, and one that can lead the funder to conclude that your proposal contains other inaccuracies as well.

A budget may include the following areas:

- *Project or program budget*: Your grant project income and expenses
- *Library budget*: Your entire library's income and expenses, including personnel and overhead
- *In-kind contribution budget*: Donated goods and services from partners and contributors that will be used for the grant project

Be prepared to be flexible about your project budget in case the funder chooses to negotiate costs. Provide information on other funding sources and efforts to supplement your grant request, including any financial commitments or support that will be provided by your library (often called in-kind contributions). This can include office space, computers or equipment, and personnel salaries. Few funders want to support an entire project; however, like most nonprofits, libraries never have enough funding. When a library is willing to dedicate a portion of its budget to a project, this demonstrates to the funder that the initiative is important to the library and that the library is prepared to support it. This also proves your organization's commitment to the project and provides indications of future sustainability. Funders value matching funds and support from other sources, so include partners' contributions as well. Other income may include individual contributions, a special fundraising event, or grants from more than one source. Each possible revenue source should be included in the budget.

If the funder gives no specifications regarding the budget, you should make sure to include all expenses, including personnel, direct project costs, and administrative expenditures.

- *Personnel expenses*: This area consists of the salaries or portions of salaries for everyone at your library. If you are including just the grant project personnel expenses, you will include everyone who will have a role working on the project. Some funders will allow you to include payroll taxes and benefits, such as insurance. If you are hiring contractors, consultants, evaluators, or trainers who will be working specifically on this project, you can include either the flat fee or hourly wage that you will be paying them.
- *Direct project expenses*: These can include project-related travel, supplies and materials, advertising and marketing, space rentals and equipment fees, photocopies, postage fees, and books.
- *Overhead or administrative costs*: These are part of your annual budget, regardless of whether your library implements the grant project. They include costs associated with buildings, utilities, telecommunication, insurance, taxes, security systems, and maintenance. Some funders won't cover overhead costs, while others will specify a flat percentage. Depending on the funder, personnel costs may be included as overhead as well. If your library is part of a larger organization, overhead costs may already be determined; for example, universities may have a set overhead percentage established for federal grant purposes.

Generally, funders expect to see a balanced budget for a project, so include both income and expenses. You may be able to include a budget narrative to explain any items that aren't immediately clear or to describe and justify specific items, relating each budget item to the grant activity it supports. See the budget worksheets in part III (pp. 178–180) for example budget forms. Further project budget details are included in chapter 3 as well.

Evaluation Process

The project evaluation plan introduced in chapter 3 (see Step 11: Create an Evaluation Plan, pp. 54–60) will be helpful for this section. Evaluation is a method to examine, monitor, and determine the effectiveness of a project or activity. Evaluation aids in determining grant achievements, outputs, and outcomes and with communicating those results to the funders and to your community. Evaluation can show what you've accomplished and whether you are spending staff time, resources, and energies on projects that are making a difference. In the evaluation component of your grant application, show how your evaluation will demonstrate what your project accomplishes, through outputs and outcomes. Think about how to measure whether you've been successful. Will it be helpful to collect statistics on how technology is used or to survey users on how technology classes have changed their lives? Your evaluation should yield results that show that your grant project made a difference. This will be valuable information to share with your funders and also to communicate and prove worth to your community.

Remember that evaluation shouldn't just be done at the end of the grant project. There may be baseline data that need to be collected before a project is begun and also throughout the duration of the grant period. A combination of outcome-based and output-based evaluation processes can be done on a midterm basis so that adjustments can be made. Some funders will require a midterm report and/or final report, and you may need to provide updates such as these:

- Quantitative information about the number of classes and participants, technology use, collections and materials (purchase and circulation), collaborations, and budget expenditures
- Qualitative data, including ongoing impact stories, lessons learned, and media relations

Also, think about the fact that some outcomes may not be achieved by the end of a grant but may come about over time. This is especially true when using outcome-based evaluation methods. There are short-term outcomes that may happen as part of grant activities, such as changes in skills, attitudes, and knowledge. However, it may be some months after a grant that medium-term outcomes, such as changes in behavior and decision making, occur. And it could take a year or longer for long-term outcomes, such as the changes in status or life condition, to come about. Most grants projects will focus on measuring short-term and medium-term outcomes.

It is important to know what funders expect when it comes to evaluation. Many funders specify the evaluation requirements for their grants; some may require specific evaluation techniques, such as outcome measures, or they may also want quantitative data on programs, collection usage, or budget reports. Some funders require an outside evaluator and will provide funding to hire someone.

Funders usually specify the methods they require for evaluation. Make sure you review the chapter 3 section Key Considerations for Writing an Evaluation Plan (see p. 59). If you have questions regarding evaluation, contact the funder, as this is often an important part of the grant requirements.

Most funders are very interested in ensuring that the funding and resources that they provide are used for a successful and intended purpose. Conducting a well-done evaluation can help sustain the partnership you have developed with your funder.

Appendix

Supporting materials are often arranged in an appendix. Find out what documents and materials are desired or allowed. These materials can endorse the project and the library, include strategic plans and certifications, provide proof of past successes, offer details about project personnel, consultants, and board members, or include statistical information. Funders may want financial statements, annual budgets, proof of tax exemption, or subject matter information.

Endorsements from supporting or partnering organizations can also be included. Find support for your proposal from partners, other types of libraries, politicians, professionals, local government agencies, or public officials. The state librarian or the state library association president might be willing to write a letter of support for a large grant. Endorsements are especially important for federal funding.

Policies about the inclusion of supporting materials differ widely among funders. Whether to allow them usually depends on how the materials contribute to a reviewer's evaluation of the proposals. Restrictions are often based on volume, bias, and relevance. Be prepared to invest the time to collect resources, document capability, update a résumé, and obtain letters or reports. Documents may include the following:

- Letters of support
- Letters of agreement
- List of board members or trustees, with titles
- Library's annual budget
- Library's mission statement
- Library's most recent accomplishments
- List of other sources of funding
- Copy of your 501(c)(3) certification
- Any additional information about your library that will help the funder determine your ability to succeed (e.g., press clippings, service brochures, statistics, staff awards)
- Curricula vitae (CVs) or résumés of participating staff members, including this information:

  - Education: degrees, fields of study, institutions, locations
  - Professional work experience: positions, including institutions and locations
  - Honors and awards
  - Relevant publications
  - Qualifications and responsibilities associated with the grant

Authorized Signatures

Authorized signatures are usually required. Proposals may be rejected for lack of a specified signature. Be sure to allow the time to acquire all needed signatures. Particularly in universities or large metropolitan settings, acquiring signatures can take some time. The last thing you want to find out is that a necessary signatory is on vacation the week your proposal is due. You may also need signatures from your board of directors or from your city's fiscal office.

Submitting Your Application

Your proposal may be judged against some major criteria using some type of rubric or scoring system. The first thing we recommended that you should have done with your application guidelines was to highlight all the questions you needed to answer and all the materials you needed to include. Add these items to your Grant Submission Checklist (see figure 6.2), if you haven't already. When you are ready to submit your entire application, turn to your checklist and go through it carefully, item by item, to make sure that you have followed all the directions and guidelines. You want to double-check that you have included everything the funder requested.

You don't want your application disqualified on a technicality. For instance, be sure that you have not single-spaced the application when the funder specified that the application must be double-spaced; included brochures about your library programs in the appendix when they clearly stated not to include an appendix; or overlooked the lobbying form and forgot to include it in a federal application. After all this hard work, you don't want your application to be tossed into the recycling bin for reasons like these. You may think that funders should just overlook such little details, but following the guidelines can be one of the most important steps toward success.

Funders eliminate applications that don't comply with their guidelines all the time. It makes their jobs easier by leaving them with fewer applications to read. This practice also eliminates candidates who don't follow directions. Usually funders have many more worthy applications than they can possibly fund. They don't have the time to deal with applicants who don't comply with the instructions. Also, they don't want to give money to an organization that cannot follow directions. So, if you want the funder to read your proposal, follow the instructions and use the checklist.

Carefully go through your application with your checklist on hand and check off every item as you make sure it is in place. Once everything is checked, you can seal the envelope and head for the post office or other delivery service or submit online. Using the option of delivery confirmation, a signature upon delivery, or some kind of tracking number can be helpful so that you know when the proposal has been delivered, and that it hasn't just disappeared without a trace after all your hard work.

Confirmation of Submission

Now, take a deep breath and congratulate yourself for a job well done! Wait one week, and then contact the funding source to make sure that the funder received your proposal if you haven't received an e-mail confirmation or other form of communication by then. Validate that you are the contact person for your proposal and ensure that the funder has your correct phone number and e-mail. Let the funder know that you want to be notified about the status, evaluation, and outcome of your proposal. Keep in mind that it may be months before decisions are made, so don't expect to hear news soon. You just want to confirm receipt.

A funder might contact you to ask questions or to clarify information in your proposal. Getting a call or an e-mail from the funder during the proposal evaluation process is a good sign; it means you are still in the running and that the funder is interested enough in your proposal to request more information. Keep your project and proposal files organized and easy to access so you can promptly answer any question a funder may have.

You can also request feedback about your proposal's strengths and weaknesses, although this information is sometimes unavailable, especially with a large volume of submissions. This may also be useful if you choose to approach the same funder again, or if you decide to contact another funder with the same project idea. More discussion on this topic appears in the next chapter.

FIGURE 6.2

GRANT SUBMISSION CHECKLIST

☐ The funder is interested in receiving my proposal.

☐ This proposal reflects the funder's areas of interest.

☐ We have followed the instructions and guidelines of the funder's specifications.

☐ Our proposal meets the page/word limits.

☐ The font type and size are correct.

☐ The margin size is correct.

☐ The line spacing is correct.

☐ We have used the specified type of paper, if indicated.

☐ We did not bind the proposal unless we were told we could.

☐ We sent the correct number of copies and the original; we also retained a copy for ourselves and copies were made for partners and supporters.

☐ We included letters of support.

☐ We have the required signatures.

☐ The proposal components are titled and compiled in the order specified.

- Title sheet
- Cover letter
- Table of contents
- Proposal summary
- Organizational overview
- Statement of needs

- Project description
- Timeline
- Budget request
- Evaluation process
- Appendix

☐ The cover letter explains the project and states the total cost of the project, the amount expected from other sources, and the amount requested.

☐ The project description specifies the need that will be met and how people will benefit.

☐ The project description tells the whole story of our project in clear, understandable language.

☐ The objectives are measurable.

☐ The methodology explains how the objectives will be met.

☐ The timeline includes all major activities and who will do them.

☐ The evaluation plan measures the degree to which the objectives and outcomes are met.

☐ The project includes partners and reflects community involvement.

☐ The budget is reasonable and the calculations are correct.

☐ The project is sustainable.

☐ Adequate personnel are identified in the proposal to do the project.

☐ Adequate resources are available to do the project.

☐ Our library has the capacity to do the project.

☐ The proposal contains no jargon or acronyms.

☐ If attachments are included, we have confirmed that the funder allows them.

☐ The proposal has been proofread by an impartial person.

FIGURE 6.2

GRANT SUBMISSION CHECKLIST

(continued from previous page)

☐ The proposal is clear and easy to understand by someone outside the grant team.

☐ Letters of agreement from partners and letters of support from supporters are included, if allowed.

☐ We have met the deadline.

☐ The proposal looks professional.

Now, carefully go through your application with your checklist and check off every item as you make sure it is in place. Once everything is checked, you may seal the envelope and head for the post office.

☐ The proposal was submitted on _____ .

☐ We have a dated receipt or confirmation that the proposal was submitted.

Getting Funded and Implementing the Project

In this final phase of the Grant Process Cycle, you discover if your grant is awarded. We've included a list of the most common reasons projects aren't funded, so that you can hopefully avoid disappointment. Also realize that the grant process itself is valuable in other aspects as well. The steps to developing the proposal are valuable for seeking any kind of funding, not only grant funding. If you do receive funding, it is time to celebrate, thank the funder, and then begin the implementation work of the grant project, including evaluation and project management activities.

After You Submit Your Application

The processes that funders use to review and evaluate proposals vary widely. Some funders send proposals to reviewers who rate them based on a predetermined scoring system. Other systems for evaluating proposals may include review committees or panels of government officials, experts in a specific field, and community-based reviewers. Or it might be a multiphase process during which your proposal is first rated by an expert in projects like yours—such as literacy programs—and then rated by a foundation advisory board. If the funder's proposal evaluation method is not outlined in the grant guidelines, you should be able to find out this information by calling your contact at the funding agency. It sometimes helps to know the funder's timeline, so you will have an idea about when to expect to hear from them about whether your project has been funded. You don't need to be anticipating a response right away if it will be two months before the funder makes a decision about which projects to fund. It is not unusual for funders to contact applicants to ask questions or to clarify information in a proposal. Getting a call or e-mail from the funder during the proposal evaluation process is a good sign; it means you are still in the running and that the funder is interested enough in your proposal to request more information. Keep your project and proposal files organized and close at hand so you can answer quickly and effectively without rifling through drawers of files and piles of paper. Funders are often busy people and they want to complete the selection process in a timely and efficient manner. If you tell them you will "get back to them on

THE GRANT PROCESS CYCLE

Plan for Success

Design Winning Grant Projects

Research Funders and Grant Opportunities

Create the Winning Proposal

Implement, Evaluate, Continue

that" or you don't promptly know the answers to their questions, you may compromise your chances of success. This is not to say that your proposal will be discredited; but it may indicate to the funder that you are not very well organized, that you are not very familiar with the details of your project, or that it will be difficult to work with you.

You may get a call about the budget or a specific activity or objective in your project. Or you may receive a list of questions that the reviewers want you to answer in writing prior to making their decision. Take care of these things promptly and follow up with the funder to make sure the funder received your responses, and that you have answered all questions to the funder's satisfaction. If you have been contacted with questions or a request for clarification, after you have responded, confirm that the funder has everything requested. This is your responsibility.

When Your Project Gets Funded

Funders may notify you that they have decided to fund your project by letter, e-mail, or phone call. The first thing to do after you are notified that your project has been funded is to thank your funder! Write a brief letter or note on behalf of the grant team expressing thanks to the funder for supporting your project and excitement about implementing the project. Assure the funder that you are anticipating a project that will successfully meet specific needs in your community.

Next, inform your team members about their success, congratulate them for a job well done, and honor their hard work by celebrating together. Remember to include your partners and supporters in the celebration. It doesn't have to be a major event or cost a lot of money. It can be as simple as cake and ice cream during an afternoon break. It is important to acknowledge everyone whose hard work made the proposal a success.

Once the funder clears you to make an announcement, let the community know about your success. Send a press release to the local papers and other media and to state and regional library publications. This is a good time to call for volunteers if your project will require them. People will be excited about becoming involved in the project at this beginning stage.

You may be required to sign a contract that stipulates the conditions of the grant. Be aware that the amount you are awarded may not be the amount you requested. The scope of work the funder has agreed to fund may not exactly match the scope of work you proposed. Reporting requirements may have changed or may not be what you expected. Make sure you understand the terms of the grant contract and the work the funder expects you to do for the funds awarded to you. If you need additional funding to successfully implement your project, secure all necessary funding before you announce that your project has been funded.

Review your budget, especially if it has been a long time between submitting your proposal and the notification of your award. Check salaries and benefits costs, technology and equipment costs, rental fees, and other dollar amounts that may have fluctuated since you submitted your proposal. If there are changes, contact the funder immediately. The funder may ask you to readjust items within your budget, totaling the same dollar amount. In other words, the funder may fund your project only for the amount you requested even if actual costs have risen. Or the funder may be in a position to fund the entire project, including higher cost adjustments. If you find the project will cost less than you proposed, get the funder's approval to use the excess funds to support your project in other ways. If you do readjust your budget, make sure this is reflected in your project activities. For instance, if personnel hours are not funded at the requested level due to higher personnel or benefits costs, this will reduce the activities they can be expected to accomplish. Be sure you are comfortable with what is in the grant contract and that it makes sense to you, especially if it differs from your proposed project and budget. Your authorizing agent will most likely need to sign the grant contract, and then you can return the signed contract to the funder.

What to Do If Your Project Is Not Funded

If your project is not funded, contact the program officer and ask for feedback on your proposal. When proposal reviewers read proposals, they take notes and write comments. These comments are compiled for the final review that determines which projects are funded and which ones are denied. If available, these comments will be valuable to you as you write your next proposal. Some funders will also offer follow-up phone calls to give personalized feedback. They will often tell you how you can make improvements or add clarity and also let you know which parts of your proposal were done well.

Remember to put these comments and the denial of funding in perspective. You may have written an outstanding proposal by most standards. If the funder had the resources to fund only a fraction of the proposals submitted, even some excellent proposals had to be denied. It is possible that the same proposal might have been funded if submitted to a funder with more resources. Also, proposal reviewers are humans who come with their own biases, preferences, and opinions. Judging grant proposals is by nature a subjective activity. The same proposal read by a different team of reviewers may have been funded.

Putting things into perspective does not mean that your proposal doesn't require some work. Read the reviewers' comments and get opinions from people you know who are not involved with your library or the proposed project. Sometimes an impartial reader can see things that you cannot because you are so close to it.

Common Reasons Why Projects Are Not Funded

- *The project does not match the purpose of the grant.* Thoroughly research the purpose of the grant and the funder's priorities and interests. Make sure your project matches them before applying for funding.
- *The applicant is not located in the funder's geographic area.* Read the guidelines carefully for geographical limitations. Some funders only fund projects in their own geographic area or in areas where they have business locations.
- *The proposal does not adhere to the guidelines.* Read the application information and proposal guidelines very carefully and follow them exactly. Then read them again. Before you submit your proposal, read the instructions one last time to make sure you have followed all the requirements. Meet the deadlines.

- *The proposal is poorly written.* Get help writing the proposal if you need it. Write clearly and succinctly. Eliminate jargon and acronyms. Spell-check your proposal and use correct grammar and punctuation.
- *The budget doesn't add up.* Check and double-check your math. Don't inflate prices. Ask only for what you need to implement your project.
- *The proposal is disorganized or difficult to understand.* Take the time and effort to prepare your proposal in a professional manner. Have friends and people with experience in the field critique the proposal before you submit it. Make sure that the purpose of the project is clear and that impartial readers understand what it is you want to accomplish.
- *The grant request is not within the funding range.* Research the average size of grants awarded by the funder and don't request amounts significantly out of that range. Be realistic.
- *The funder doesn't know enough about your organization,* such as whether you are a credible and trustworthy partner. If possible, set up an interview or phone call before submitting the proposal and have board members and other funded organizations help you establish a relationship to give you credibility. Write an organizational overview that clearly explains who you are. Provide documented evidence that you are up to implementing the project you are proposing. Include your long-range plan and how your project relates to it.
- *The necessity for your project and its potential impact are not clear.* Demonstrate the need for your project in the community with real information and data. Clearly identify the people who will benefit from your project, your target audience, and how the project will improve their quality of life. Don't base your proposal on the things you need. Your aim is to stress the importance of your project, but not to sound like you are in crisis mode.
- *The budget is unrealistic or inaccurate.* Never guess at the cost of items in your budget. Do not rely on sales or limited-time offers for an accurate price. When it comes time to purchase the equipment, a sale price may no longer be available and the new price may even be higher than the regular price. Do not forget supplies like paper, pens, toner, and copying costs when preparing your budget. Be realistic about the cost of personnel benefits and taxes. Only promise what can realistically be delivered for the amount requested.
- *No partners or collaborators are indicated.* Make sure your proposal clearly shows that you have support from other organizations and that they are involved in your project. If allowed, you should include a letter of support from all partnering organizations in your proposal. It needs to be obvious to the reviewer that the partnering organizations are aware of the project, that there is partner buy-in, and that they have agreed to actively participate.
- *No clear and relevant evaluation plan is evident.* Evaluation is a critical component of any proposal. Numbers and statistics alone don't effectively evaluate a project. Outcome-based evaluation will measure how your project will change the behavior, skills, attitude, knowledge, status, or life condition of the people your project serves.
- *The project isn't sustainable.* Most funders require you to show how you intend to support your project after the grant ends. Add a section to the proposal about your plans for self-sufficiency and develop a long-term strategy. Perhaps

a partner organization is willing to take the lead at the conclusion of the current funding.

Don't be discouraged. It is not uncommon, especially in the federal arena, for funders to receive more money after funding the first round of applicants. This means that they must go to the next level—those applicants that just missed getting funded the first time. If this happens to you, you must be ready to think and act quickly. If you have been turned down and you are looking for other funding, you may get a call from the funder to whom you originally submitted your proposal asking if you are still seeking funding for your project. Even if you have received other funding for your project in the meantime, be ready with ideas for a second phase of your project, a sustainability component, or a similar project you have planned for the future that could use funding. Talk to the funder about the possibilities. Most funders who are interested in your proposal will be open to reconfiguring your project, talking about your project's current funding needs, or discussing other related projects you have planned.

Implementing the Project

If your project has been funded, it is time for the implementation phase to begin. A project implementation team can be very helpful in making sure your project is a success. This team can include staff, volunteers, and your grant partners. A team leader or project manager should oversee this work. A good project manager is a good planner and also able to be flexible and adaptable.

Grant Project Management

Grant project management is just like managing any other type of project, such as library events or library programming. Project management is the process of managing people, resources, and time. The WebJunction *Competency Index for the Library Field*, edited by Betha Gutsche and Brenda Hough (2014, 33), lists three main characteristics of a successful project leader:

- "Employs sound project management principles and procedures in the planning and implementation of programs and services"
- "Leads work teams with clear direction and effective communication"
- "Monitors and evaluates projects and adapts as needed"

Thus, there are four essential components of grant project management:

1. Communication
2. Team building
3. Planning
4. Evaluation

Good communication and team building are essential throughout the grant project life cycle. You need ongoing communication with your team, using multiple methods (e-mail, meetings, one-on-one check-ins, etc.) to clarify and confirm understanding so that project goals are met. Make a point to communicate with each team member on a regular basis to make sure all are aware of expectations. Get input and feedback from each team member. Be open to new ideas and get your team into the habit of measuring ideas against the grant project goals. Encourage team members to discuss project activities, work together to solve problems, and keep you apprised of their progress. Avoid micromanaging or holding unnecessary meetings. Acknowledge and resolve problems immediately. Ask your team, "What can I do to create an environment that will help you complete your tasks?" Then identify and supply the tools and resources the team members need to do their jobs. Make sure you provide constructive feedback and acknowledge tasks that are well done. Celebrate milestones and make sure that ownership of the project is shared by all team members.

A lot of your planning should have been completed during the project planning phase. You will need to examine the project goals, outcomes, and outputs and make sure the timeline and budget are still applicable. Then you are ready to plan your tasks. You may need some project management tools, such as Microsoft Excel or Microsoft Project, Basecamp, or other methods, for tracking the who, what, when, where, and how of your grant project. Your timeline should have established milestones and project evaluation methods. Identify all the tasks, who should be involved, how you will measure results, and all deadlines. Create a chart or other method to keep track of all tasks. Every task should have an associated deadline. IMLS, in association with Indiana University–Purdue University Indianapolis (IUPUI), has created an online tutorial, *Shaping Outcomes*, that uses outcome-based planning to clarify all the various components of a grant project and measure changes in the target audience. Visit the website (www .shapingoutcomes.org) if you'd like to learn more about this method.

The final phase of project management is evaluation. Build periodic evaluations into the duration of your project. Doing so will help you to know when you have reached your goal—or when you have fallen short of it. You should have already determined what success looks like and what evaluation methods you are going to use. If not, decide when and what you will evaluate and identify who is responsible for this part of the project. Finally, have a discussion about what worked well and what you could do better by bringing team members together to celebrate and debrief.

Implementation Basics

Make sure you complete the following:

1. *Contact your funder.* After celebrating your success, call your program officer to get reacquainted or to introduce yourself if you haven't already spoken with the program officer. Confirm that the funder has the contact person's name and the correct phone, fax, and e-mail information. Make yourself available. Ask any questions you may have, and begin to develop a working relationship with your program officer. Ask the program officer to call if any questions or concerns arise. The program officer can be very helpful to you as you begin project implementation and throughout the life of your project.

2. *Establish a baseline for evaluation.* It is important to begin implementing the evaluation process for your project as soon as you receive funding. You should have already planned your evaluation methodology as part of planning your project. After securing funding, but before you begin project implementation, you must establish a baseline or starting point against which you will measure your success. This may require conducting an assessment of the current knowledge or skills of your target audience or establishing the state of technology or equipment in your library prior to the start of your project. You may need to do a pre-project survey or an updated needs assessment to establish an accurate baseline. Your community needs assessment may have taken place months ago, and recent changes in your population demographics must be taken into account. Where you start depends on the nature of your project. Reread your objectives and the evaluation methodology described in your proposal and start working on this right away. Your project cannot begin until you have established a baseline for your evaluation.

3. *Hire personnel and assign tasks.* If you need to hire staff, post or advertise the positions as soon as possible. In some organizations, this takes some time, so you will want to take care of this right away. If your project will employ consultants, you may want to issue an RFP for the scope of work you need accomplished. If personnel changes occurred in your organization since you submitted the proposal, introduce new personnel to the project and clarify their roles. Make sure they understand your expectations and adjust their project responsibilities based on individual strengths. When you add new project responsibilities to their workloads, you must remove other responsibilities so as not to overburden their time commitment in your organization.

4. *Purchase equipment, materials, and supplies.* After the positions are advertised, begin to purchase equipment, technology, materials, supplies, and any other items you need for your project. Since you confirmed costs in your budget right after being notified that you were funded, this is the best time to purchase—before costs fluctuate again.

5. *Designate a workspace.* Your project may need to have a "home" and a physical place for project personnel to work in close proximity to one another. Give your project the recognition it deserves by defining a place for it to thrive. You want your project staff to be able to communicate easily as they make your project come to life.

6. *Update the timeline.* Update the project timeline to include each detailed step, specific personnel responsible for each activity, and inclusive dates for all activities. It is sometimes helpful to post the timeline in a prominent place where project personnel will see it daily.

7. *Clarify the funder's reporting requirements.* Familiarize yourself with your funder's reporting requirements so that you gather the right information, you are ready to prepare your reports when they are due, and you send them to the funder on time. Some funders require one final evaluation at the conclusion of the project, while others require periodic reports throughout the life of the project. Your project evaluation should be based on the original purpose of the project and indicate the extent to which that purpose was achieved. If

you didn't accomplish all the grant objectives, it does not necessarily mean the project was a failure. Valuable lessons may have been learned or the population served may have been positively affected in ways other than those planned. The evaluation should outline any unexpected results or consequences and should also specify how the grant will affect future projects. Evaluation reports that are due periodically throughout the project will present opportunities for you to adjust any project components that are not working as expected.

8. *Begin evaluation activities.* If you based your evaluation plan on outcome-based evaluation, as discussed in chapter 3, the outcomes should be used to evaluate the impact on the population served, as indicated by change in knowledge, attitude, behavior, status, skills, or life condition. If you are doing public library programming as part of your grant project, the surveys and tools available from the Public Library Association's Project Outcome may be useful. Visit the website (www.projectoutcome.org) if you'd like to learn more about this process. Include any relevant information gained from your evaluation, such as data collected from focus groups or surveys, and statistical data. To enhance your evaluation, include qualitative data, such as stories or anecdotes, interviews, and case studies that illustrate how individuals benefited from the project. The evaluation must also report on how the grant money was used. This report should correspond with the budget agreed upon by you and the funder. This may be the original budget appearing in your proposal or an amended budget approved by your funder. Any deviations from this budget should be explained. Here is a sample of the kinds of information funders request in a grant evaluation or progress report:

- Purpose achieved
- Summary of outcomes/results achieved
- Report of expenditures
- Future plans for the grant project
- Lessons learned/impact on future projects
- Telling the story of the people helped
- Publications or presentations connected to the grant
- Honors or awards received as a result of the grant

Whether you are implementing a project that was funded or you are ready to research more grant opportunities for a project that still needs funding, your next step is to review the Grant Process Cycle you have just completed. It is important to identify what you can do to improve, where you excelled, what steps in the process need more attention from you, and what you would do exactly the same way. The next chapter provides more details about reviewing and continuing the process.

Reviewing and Continuing the Process

Congratulations on completing your first round of the Grant Process Cycle!

If you have had success by winning grant funding for your project the first time around, you are now in the initial stages of project implementation. Or if you were not successful this time, you may be ready to try again. Either way, this is the time for you to review and continue the grant process.

Debrief and Review

Take some time now to meet with your project planning team and your grant team to debrief. Often, it takes experiencing the entire process at least once before you can really understand how the process works, what the process requires of you, the value of going through each step, or what results to expect. Review the process and ask yourselves honestly, "How did it go?" Use the Debrief and Review Checklist (see figure 8.1) to prompt discussion; the checklist is also included in part III (see p. 197) and online (www.alaeditions.org/webextras).

Reviewing your experiences at this stage in the process will give you an opportunity to learn from your successes and failures and to make the necessary improvements or adjustments for your next attempt. Whatever you can learn at any stage in the process can only help you to do better the next time around. As you can see, this process is never done; there is no last step. However, the best time to look back on a project is after you have just completed a Grant Process Cycle.

After debriefing and reviewing, continue with the grant process. There may be some steps that you can go through quickly now that you have your strategic plan in place, your community profile and needs assessment have been updated, and you have discovered and designed several projects.

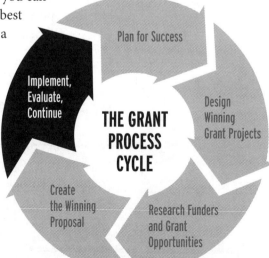

FIGURE 8.1

DEBRIEF AND REVIEW CHECKLIST

- ☐ Did we remain true to the strategic plan?
- ☐ Was our project designed to meet community needs?
- ☐ Did we work well as a team?
- ☐ Where did we excel as a team? Where could we improve?
- ☐ Did we delegate well?
- ☐ Is there anything we overlooked?
- ☐ What would we do differently?
- ☐ Did we forget to include a potential partner?
- ☐ Did we complete everything on time?
- ☐ Did we feel rushed getting authorized signatures, submitting the proposal before the deadline, getting proper approvals, or gathering letters of support?
- ☐ Was it stressful? How could we reduce the stress next time?
- ☐ If we were successful this time, why were we successful?
- ☐ If we were unsuccessful this time, why were we unsuccessful? What were the funder's comments about our proposal and how can we improve?

Keep Your Project Plans Up-to-Date

The grant process is always aligned with your library's strategic plan and project plans. Therefore, when you update your strategic plan or you are aware of new community needs, you must build these changes into your existing project plans or create new project plans. If you update a funded project, make sure to contact the funder about changes to the plan before you proceed. When you update and review your project plans continuously, as changes occur in your community and in your strategic plan, this becomes a matter of course, a normal part of your job. When you keep your plans up-to-date, you are always ready for a new grant opportunity. Creating strategic plans, performing needs assessments, and designing project plans can be overwhelming tasks when you do them only once every three to five years. Librarians who do not stay current usually avoid pursuing grants because "it is too much work." Help yourself out and give your library a chance to win grants by updating your plans frequently.

Update Grant Proposal Components

Some grant proposal components can be updated periodically and kept in a file ready to go into a new proposal when the time is right. Doing this will save time, allowing you to concentrate on new ideas and spend less time gathering facts. As you update your strategic plan, community needs assessment, and project plans, keep current versions of these on file.

- *Library profile and/or organizational overview*: Update your library profile and organizational overview as you would your résumé. Add new achievements, events and programming, leadership, board members, and key staff members. If your library's mission or vision has changed, make these changes in your library profile. Updated budget figures can illustrate funding trends in your library, and new anecdotes, success stories, and endorsements from satisfied customers can keep this component fresh and current.
- *Statement of needs*: The statement of needs can be adjusted as your community needs assessment is updated. You may have several of these statements, depending on your particular community and various grant projects.
- *Community profile*: Your community profile can be updated as your municipality, college or university, or school or organization changes and updates information about its residents, students, employees, or people served. When new census data is released, incorporate this information into your community profile. Note any current articles about your community's status, such as unemployment rates, high school dropout rates, health concerns, or illiteracy, that are published in your local newspaper.

Participate in Professional Development and Continuing Education

There is always more to learn about grants and proposal writing, so stay current and up-to-date by taking tutorials, classes, and webinars whenever you can.

- Attend workshops on researching grant opportunities or preparing grant proposals given by your organization, university, or municipality.
- Attend individual foundation information sessions where you will learn about specific foundations' interests, priorities, and preferences and their funding opportunities, and have an opportunity to ask questions and develop new relationships.
- Attend proposal-writing workshops given by your local community foundation, community college, state humanities council, or regional library system.
- Take an online course, tutorial, or webinar or attend classroom training at the Foundation Center (http://foundationcenter.org). You can learn about proposal writing, proposal budgeting, funding research, corporate giving, and more. Here are some other educational opportunities:

  - The Grantsmanship Center (www.tgci.com) offers an intensive five-day Grantsmanship Training Program in various locations across the United States.
  - Your state library may offer workshops or guidance on grant research, proposal writing, or how to apply for LSTA and other funding that they offer.

- Federal agencies often offer free regional proposal-writing workshops and/or informational sessions on upcoming funding opportunities. They provide tips for writing proposals and how to be more competitive. These workshops and sessions are usually held in various locations nationwide and include representatives from the agencies who can answer your questions.

- Attend workshops on grants research, proposal writing, and project planning at your state library association conference, regional library association conference, or national library conferences, such as those held by ALA or PLA.

Foster Partnerships and Build Relationships

The best time to create and nurture partnerships is when you are not under pressure to write a proposal or find partners for a grant with a tight application deadline. It is best to continuously work on these relationships as a matter of course. Make a point of meeting people outside your organization, leaders in the community, and key people in agencies or businesses who are doing activities that relate to the projects you have planned. Get out of your library building and attend community meetings, join community groups, volunteer to give talks to local groups, or visit local schools. Be visible.

Tell others in the community about your new ideas and plans. Speak at civic club meetings and other community organization events about your goals, the community needs you would like to address, and prospective projects. Volunteer to help with your partners' or potential partners' fundraising events, or create an e-mail distribution list announcing your accomplishments.

Build relationships with potential funders. If you have already received a grant, recognize your funder by using the funder's name and logo on project materials, distribute press releases, spread the word in your newsletter, and include links to articles about the funder on your library's website. Invite the funder to special events, and recognize the funder at your annual awards program. Make sure to thank your funders and keep them updated about the progress of your project or about special accomplishments related to the project they funded. Send them publicity materials and copies of articles about your library and the funded project.

Join Fundraising Groups and Associations

Join your state or local chapter of the Association of Fundraising Professionals (www.afpnet.org). You will meet others in your community who are experienced fundraisers and proposal writers, and you will be invited to association events that may include workshops about grants and proposal writing or talks by local funders. You will have the opportunity to network and join a supportive group with others like you who are searching for grants, writing proposals, and securing project funds.

Be a Grant Reviewer

Consider volunteering to be a grant reviewer. You can learn a lot about the grant process and how to build stronger proposals while also building relationships with funders and making new connections with other nonprofits.

Continue to Do the Research

In chapter 5, we stressed the importance of staying up-to-date with new grant opportunities using blogs, current awareness services, electronic newsletters, periodicals, online discussion groups, and RSS feeds. This is the time to update your subscriptions and ensure this part of your research is current. Refer to chapter 5 for detailed information about these resources.

Library Grants Blog

We maintain a blog that lists national grant opportunities that are suitable for libraries. We do the searching for you! Subscribe to the RSS feed and you will receive new opportunities as they are posted. The blog is updated as we discover new grant announcements. We do not post local, regional, or state-specific grant announcements.

◊◊◊◊◊◊◊◊◊◊◊◊◊◊◊◊◊◊

The time you take to debrief and review, keep your plans and proposal components up-to-date, participate in professional development and continuing education, foster partnerships and build relationships, become involved in fundraising groups, learn best practices, and stay current is an investment in yourself and in the library.

Tips for Grant Success

1. Focus on People

The most important thing to remember is that grants are about people. Grants are not about getting money or things. Funders want to make a difference in the lives of people by funding projects that accomplish goals that match their priorities. Focus on how the grant project will help people and meet their needs, not the money or the "stuff" you will buy for the library. Involve as many people as possible throughout the grant process. Always ask your target audience for feedback and *listen* to what they say. Remember that funders are people, too. They are there to help you better serve your community.

Talk with them about their organizations' interests and priorities, and develop good working relationships with them. Keep them up-to-date on your library, even after your grant projects are completed.

2. Plan Ahead

The most important aspect of success with grants is careful planning and project development before you write a proposal. Funders often say they receive many proposals that are full of great ideas; however, practical plans, strategies for implementation, and clear goals and objectives are often missing. Grant work must begin with planning, using your library's mission, strategic plan, and needs assessments as a foundation. Once you review this information, validate a real need your library can help address and brainstorm solutions. You are then ready to determine a grant project idea. By planning and having a project in mind before you begin researching funding sources and selecting specific funders and grants, writing the grant proposal will be much easier. Funders prefer well-planned grant projects.

3. Know What You Want to Accomplish

An effective proposal describes a project that has goals and includes strategies for implementing the project. Proposals are not a list of what the library needs. Your proposal must say exactly what you will accomplish and how you will get there. Be specific about broad goals, measurable objectives, outcomes, and strategies. Be clear about how people will benefit and how the project will make a difference in their lives. Incorporate these goals into your conversations with library staff, board members, community leaders, and others. The library's goals and, thus, the grant project goals are part of your purpose or mission, not just extras you do temporarily so you can get money or buy things for the library.

Often libraries offer programming, such as summer reading or computer classes, but never really think about what they are ultimately trying to accomplish or the results they want for people. If you don't know what you are trying to do, there is no way to know if you have been successful. Do you want reading skill levels to increase? Adults to be promoted at their jobs due to increased technology knowledge? Or more children to attend summer reading? There is no sense in offering programs when you don't know why you are offering them. Funders don't often give grants for projects that have no goals.

Evaluation plans are necessary to determine if you accomplished what you set out to do. How do you know if you truly made a difference? Measure your progress and report your incremental achievements as you go along. Don't wait until the end of the grant project to see if you got it right. Benchmarks that are realistic, are measured monthly and quarterly, and involve both quantitative and qualitative measurements are very important. Often, knowing if you've been successful starts with knowing where you started. Evaluations and surveys should be conducted prior to project start dates and then repeated. Know how you are going to evaluate your grant project—throughout the Grant Process Cycle.

4. Meet Community Needs

You must clearly know how the funds will be used. Target your programs and projects so that funders will know exactly what you will be doing with their money, goods, or services.

Your project should not just be a good idea; it should meet a true need in your community. This grant should make a difference, and you need to demonstrate how it will do so in your proposal. What are the concrete benefits to your community? You should identify a target audience that is an appropriate population to benefit. Libraries serve diverse populations, and this is attractive to funders if it matches their purposes as well. You should include the target audience in the project planning to ensure that your library is doing the project *with* the people you will be helping, not *to* them. Funders want to know that the people who will benefit from the project have provided input and assisted with designing the project, and that they truly welcome the project.

On a large scale, your project can have the power to affect public opinion and policy and transform your community. Even if your scope is not this extensive, the project should still have outcome potential for more than a few people. For example, a reading program for toddlers that serves only a few families will not have a broad impact on your community.

5. Be Realistic

Verify your library's organizational capacity and support. Know what you can and can't do, based on local resources, priorities, and policies. Be certain that your library can follow through and achieve the results intended for your project; otherwise, you should not be applying for a grant. Funders need to be sure your library is competent and that the leadership can be trusted to carry out their intentions and truly deliver what has been promised.

Your library must commit to the process and be invested in the project. Two of the most precious resources of any library are its funds and its staff. If a library is willing to dedicate a portion of those discretionary funds and staff hours to the proposed project, this signals a legitimate priority, rather than merely chasing grant dollars. Relevant staff and administrators must buy in to the project in the planning stages. Be certain to build into the project someone who will manage the project and follow through with implementation and reporting. This will not only guarantee grant compliance but also increase your chances of a successful project.

6. Ask for What You Need

Include in your budget everything your project will require. It is better to be realistic with your request than to ask for less than you need and come up short. Don't look for sales or cut back on necessary personnel because you think asking for less will increase your chances of success. This is wrong. We once reviewed grant proposals for computer laptop labs. One library asked for every part of the lab, including funding to pay for instructors for computer classes, marketing expenses, and computer tables. Another library asked for only the technology. While both libraries were fully funded, the one that asked for more got more. Know definitely what you want to do, and then ask for what you need to do it. Libraries do change lives, and we need to make sure that funders and supporters know that we are not just informational, but transformational.

7. Actively Engage

Be visible in the community, talk with others, and look locally for grant funding. The OCLC (2008, 7-5) report *From Awareness to Funding: A Study of Library Support in America* has the following important tips for pursuing funding:

> A successful library funding support campaign must:
>
> - Make the library relevant for the 21st century.
> - Instill a sense of urgency by putting the library in a competitive context for funding, alongside the public schools, fire department and police department.
> - Activate conversations about the library's importance in community infrastructure and its role in the community's future.

Spread the word about your plans. Let everyone know that you are looking for funding for a library project, and pitch them your ideas. Tell staff, board members, students, government offices, family and friends, local business leaders, teachers and academics, volunteers—anyone involved in the library or interested in library-related topics. You never know where a great contact might come from or who might be on a foundation board or know of just the right funding opportunity. Contact other libraries in your area that have received grants and ask them for advice or brainstorm on shared needs.

Get out of the library. It is important that you give the library's name, work, and achievements a voice within the community. Network, consider potential collaborators or partners in your work, provide potential donors with information and answer their questions, find out what other nonprofits are doing (e.g., to survive this economy), and make sure that you hand out your business card at every opportunity. Share your library's work and recent achievements and successes every chance that you have the floor in front of anyone outside the library. Make sure that your staff, board, and other representatives know their personal elevator speeches about your library and use them often and regularly—the best free PR and marketing that exists. Contact your community's press and other media every time your library meets a benchmark, achieves programmatic successes, or raises unprecedented support. Letting others know when your library succeeds engenders confidence in the library's leadership, confidence that the library is succeeding at its work and meeting needs in the community, and that the library isn't failing or closing anytime soon. This kind of organization attracts funding. No one wants to donate to a library that has operations, fundraising, or programming problems. Communities support success.

8. Partner and Collaborate

Collaborations and partnerships are a great way to leverage resources, share expertise, and apportion costs to tackle complex challenges. Whether you have a small or large staff, partners can also help increase your library's organizational capacity. Determine whether other groups in your community share your vision and goals. Begin collaborating with those individuals or groups before you apply for grants. Community partners, such as public agencies, businesses, or service groups, can help add validity to your proposal. Programs that are designed in isolation from the community they serve and that are devoid of partners are inclined to fail. Think carefully about other organizations that could be partners on your grant project and include them in the project planning process from the beginning.

Your relationships with funders are also a type of partnership. When you research potential funders and find that perfect fit, your goals and theirs should match like pieces of a puzzle. You should be clear about what the funder is trying to achieve, what the funder expects of your library, and what will be required throughout the grant cycle. But to truly build effective partnerships that endure, libraries need to cultivate strong relationships with funders. This means working together on an ongoing basis to share ideas and approaches to problems. The relationship requires mutual trust, honesty, and clarity, which takes time and effort to achieve.

Frequent communications, establishing personal connections, and finding creative ways to reach out to donors are all ways to build real relationships. You need to have contact with funders that goes beyond sending the proposal and final report. Send them newsletters, periodic updates, and invitations to events, so that you aren't contacting them only when you need funds. If your library gets an award or your grant project has produced something noteworthy, send them a clipping or reprint with a handwritten note. Build relationships with both current and potential donors.

9. Be Positive

Attitude, perception, and public opinion make a difference. Facts by themselves are not persuasive and do not motivate people to give. Decisions to give are often emotional. Provide fact-based, verifiable statements but include the passion you feel for the people you serve. It is an art, and there is no single way to do it. Don't be afraid to include emotions with your facts and data. After all, you are communicating with people with whom you share values and you want to persuade them to champion your project while fulfilling their cause.

A positive attitude will go a long way. Some libraries get so mired down by budget, staff, and/or space shortages that their grant applications seem like an airing of grievances rather than evidence of needs with plans for creative solutions. If you have a negative attitude, you will be communicating this to the funder in your proposal. Although you must describe your community's needs to demonstrate the reasons your library requires the funding, the purpose of the grant project you are proposing is to solve problems. Don't get stuck in the negativity of the problem but instead focus on the solution. Make sure that the application's overall message is encouraging and perhaps even inspirational. Funders have a vision of how they can help make the world a better place, and your library has the means to assist in fulfilling this exceptional goal. Remember to be grateful to the funder and to all the staff who support the grant. Celebrate any success, and always give recognition where it is due.

10. Pay Attention to the Details

When completing grant proposals or award applications, follow the guidelines explicitly and answer all the questions. Make it easy for grant reviewers to find the information requested by following the same format and headings as the application, and your proposal will be easier to read. Reviewers may have hundreds of applications to read, so don't let yours be disqualified due to a technicality. We know about someone who submitted a single-spaced proposal when the guidelines specified double-spaced, and that proposal went straight into the trash. Make it a goal to rid your proposal and documentation of typos or inaccuracies that could indicate carelessness or lack of dedication. Meet all deadlines on time or ahead of schedule. Stay aware of the details as you implement the project, carry out the evaluation, and submit your reports.

11. Be Persistent

If you don't win a grant, try, try again. One of our favorite examples of grant success comes from a library volunteer who wrote ten grants her first year. She had never written a grant before, yet she received seven of the ten—a great achievement. But what if she had written only one that wasn't funded and then gave up? Keep trying; it is all a learning process. No one is ever 100 percent successful, but librarians have a lot of advantages in the grant world, so keep writing!

Good Luck

Best of luck in your grant-writing endeavors! There is a saying that luck—and success—is what occurs when preparation meets opportunity. Plan, prepare, and then go after those grant opportunities. Continue the process and build grant work into your job. Remember that proposal writing is really about four things for which librarians are best known: conducting research, answering questions, building relationships, and serving the community.

Part II

Library Grant Success Stories

Staff Innovation Fund™

Grant Project Description

The Staff Innovation Fund™ project empowered our staff by developing their critical skills to create a more dynamic and sustainable future in Rancho Cucamonga. Young, inexperienced, and/or seasoned staff alike were included through a series of mini-grants available through a Staff Innovation Fund™. In September 2011, the Rancho Cucamonga Library received a grant from the California State Library for $50,000 to train library staff (and several city staff) in the areas of project management, creativity, partnerships, leadership, branding, communication, visioning, etc. The library then received a dedicated Innovation Fund from which staff could apply for funds to carry out projects they envisioned, created, and wanted to implement for the community. Staff attended ten training sessions and then applied (either individually or in teams) for grant funds to implement their projects. In total, ten grants were awarded to the Rancho Cucamonga Library and its partner in this project, Whittier Public Library. Whereas the training and projects were completed in September 2012, the project continues today. Once the California State Library and others saw how successful the Staff Innovation Fund™ project was, there were many requests from interested California library directors to bring it to their libraries. The state library subsequently decided to offer a Staff Innovation Fund™ to seven libraries as part of a statewide grant. Rancho Cucamonga Library was hired as a contractor to coordinate and provide training to these seven jurisdictions. The funds received for this contract have been put into an Innovation Fund for Rancho Cucamonga Library staff in order to sustain the project. Staff have already begun dreaming up new ideas for projects that will benefit the community.

Library
Rancho Cucamonga Library Services
7368 Archibald Avenue
Rancho Cucamonga, CA 91730

Contact
Michelle Perera, Library Director
michelle.perera@cityofrc.us
909-477-2720, ext. 5055

Funder
California State Library Pitch an Idea cycle

POPULATION SERVED

17,200

COLLECTION SIZE

300,000 books, DVDs, CDs, etc. Does not include digital collection.

GRANT AMOUNT

$50,000 first year, up to $350,000 annually for four jurisdictions

Number of People Who Worked on Grant Application

Two people worked on the original, but after the first part of the grant was executed (in year one), about thirty staff worked on grants and applied for grants.

Partnerships and Collaborations

There were several partnerships for the Innovation Fund grants: Animal Center, Engineering Department, high school Robotics Club, Chamber of Commerce, Department of Public Health, Developmental Centers, schools, local historical societies, and migrant farm workers.

Diverse Audiences Reached

Migrant farm workers, rural populations, Spanish-speaking communities, special needs populations, reluctant readers (therapy dogs), seniors, and homeless people

Innovative Programming Implemented

Power for miners to charge their devices; STEM (science, technology, engineering, mathematics), including robotics, minecraft, circuits, Scratch (free programming language), sensory story times for special needs children; senior fraud programming; music education, called Rock N Roll high schools; link to SLA

Key to Project/Proposal Success

Our project built capacity in the library workforce during a time of many library retirements. It was replicable in other library organizations, not just ours. It included outside partners from other agencies who attended the training and were eligible for grant funds through library partnerships. Team building and camaraderie was created among library staff.

Unexpected Outcomes

One partner was from the City Engineering Department (Rancho Cucamonga Municipal Utility) who learned about the library for the first time. As a result of the partnership, RCMU submitted a grant from the American Public Power Association's (APPA) Demonstration of Energy-Efficiency Developments (DEED) program for solar panels for the library and included $20,000 in funds to build a Renewable Energy Play and Learn Island™ for the library's children's department.

Most Difficult Part of Grant Process

Coordinating schedules with trainers, facilitators, and over thirty staff at each library each year

Advice for Other Grant Seekers

Try something different. Be true to your mission.

Most Important Element of Your Success

Showing a need and being true to your library's mission; being passionate about the library project

Credit: Michelle Perera, Library Director

The Wildcat Spot

Grant Project Description

This project will create a reading spot in an area underneath the skylight in the library. It will be a place where students can not only read but also relate to each other. It will consist of lounge seating, a coffee table, and a rug. Here they can check out and use tech resources such as an iPad Mini 3 (to be purchased with this grant) and a Kindle (a device the library already owns). The devices will allow students to access e-books on Overdrive and other e-book platforms along with the mobile versions of the district databases for research. Students will also be able to check out a charging station and popular board games for use in this space. Students can reserve this space to meet with small groups to collaborate on projects and assignments.

Library
Woodrow Wilson High School Library
100 South Glasgow Drive
Dallas, TX 75214

Contact
Valerie Tagoe, Media Specialist
vtagoe@dallasisd.org
972-502-4455

Funder
Dallas Independent School District Reading Department and the Boone Foundation

Unusual Aspect of Grant Funding
The funding for this grant came from within the school district as part of Dallas Reads, a language and literacy initiative. School librarians and teachers had the opportunity to apply for the Coolest Spot in the Room Grant. The grant awarded $1,000 grants to one elementary school teacher, a middle school teacher, a high school teacher, and a librarian.

Number of People Who Worked on Grant Application
One, just me. I am one of two librarians at my campus.

POPULATION SERVED

1,650

COLLECTION SIZE

12,354 titles

GRANT AMOUNT

$1,000

Partnerships and Collaborations

I did not partner or collaborate with another staff member. I have a vision as to what the school library can be, and I wanted to make an improvement that will make the library a comfortable and welcoming place for students to read, meet, and work.

Diverse Audiences Reached

The campus population that I serve is very diverse. We have students from a variety of racial, ethnic, and socioeconomic backgrounds. We also have a diverse staff.

Innovative Programming Implemented

The grant allowed for the purchase of furniture and equipment. I hope to use the space to teach small groups of students how to access e-books in Overdrive and other e-book platforms like MackinVia and Brytewave.

Key to Project/Proposal Success

I think the idea of having a space where students can meet, read, and play in the hope of revitalizing the library and the library program was what made the project successful.

What You Would Do Differently

I would have asked the reading department, the administrator of the grant, if I am able to use any vendor or district vendors. Since the grant was awarded in-house, so to speak, I had to use district vendors. Furniture is more expensive when it is purchased via district vendors. Hence, I was not able to purchase the iPad and board games as originally planned.

Most Difficult Part of Grant Process

The most difficult part was placing the order for the furniture purchase and having it filled. I had to contact the district's purchasing department and work with the staff in order to get the order filled due to a delay with the vendor I was working with.

Advice for Other Grant Seekers

Do your research when applying for a grant when it comes to the purchase of furniture, books, and other classroom materials. If the grant is given by the school district, find out if you are limited to working with district-approved vendors.

Most Important Element of Your Success

I think an idea that is versatile is the most important element of a successful grant—versatile in that you can detail more than one benefit of the grant. For example, this grant created not only a reading space but a space where students can collaborate and play games.

Credit: Valerie Tagoe, Media Specialist

Meet the Artist, Be the Artist: A Teaching-Artist in Residence

Grant Project Description

Local visual artist Melanie P. Brown will have a four-week residency at Skokie Public Library, during which time children grades K–8 will engage in art and creativity exercises surrounding the theme of "place." A combination of weekly drop-in events and registered workshops will engage regular library users as well as youth new to library programming settings. Partnerships with local after school groups will bring in youth who do not usually frequent the library and its programs. The events and workshops will culminate with a public celebration and exhibition of the work of the artist as well as of youth who have participated. Youth artwork will be accompanied by artist statements written by the artists. The celebration will include a collaborative artwork to which all participants can contribute.

Library
Skokie Public Library
5215 Oakton Street
Skokie, IL 60077

Contact
Amy Koester,
Youth and Family Program Coordinator
akoester@skokielibrary.info
847-324-3121

Funder
ALSC (Association for Library Service to Children) Curiosity Creates Grant, funded by Disney

Number of People Who Worked on Grant Application
Three people worked on the grant application, all library staff.

Partnerships and Collaborations
We are partnering with Y.O.U. (Youth & Opportunity United) after-school groups at our local elementary and junior high schools to bring in youth who are underserved

POPULATION SERVED
65,000

COLLECTION SIZE
500,000 print; 450,000 e-resources

GRANT AMOUNT
$7,500

in creative opportunities. We are partnering with the local parks department to display student artwork after the residency concludes.

Diverse Audiences Reached

Skokie itself is incredibly diverse (more than seventy languages spoken in local elementary schools), and our typical school-year, after-school youth audience reflects that diversity. We are reaching a different facet of our population with this grant project, however, by actively working with schools and after-school programs to identify and target youth whose opportunities to engage in creative endeavors may be limited by socioeconomic factors that result in barriers to access.

Innovative Programming Implemented

The project includes four stand-alone drop-in sessions for each age group (K–2, 3–5, 6–8) to explore core artistic concepts and skills. Participation in all sessions is not necessary, but full participation does build a fuller experience. Additionally, the in-depth artistic workshops led by a working artist represent a departure from the typical arts and crafts programs offered at the library. The culminating celebration and its collaborative painting activity represent a unique opportunity for the community to create artwork together.

Key to Project/Proposal Success

The level of collaboration in the project is key to its success, including both intralibrary collaboration (among departments) as well as collaboration with community organizations. The collaboration and sharing of ideas and insights has made the project much more successful than it would have been with any single vision.

What You Would Do Differently

At this point, we don't know that we'd have done something differently. We've used this grant process as an opportunity to prototype what a recurring Meet the Artist, Be the Artist teaching-artist residency might look like and how it would be supported at the library.

Most Difficult Part of Grant Process

The most difficult part of the grant process was the initial refining of our ideas into a cohesive project that would bring value to the community and meet a demonstrated community need.

Advice for Other Grant Seekers

Start brainstorming with a blank slate. The more ideas you can start with, the better your ultimate project will be. Use those ideas to inject your final project with aspects you might not have considered.

Most Important Element of Your Success

Regular meetings have been invaluable for this project. Since it involves so many staff in so many departments, as well as individuals outside the library, regular check-ins have been integral to everyone feeling competent and informed.

Credit: Amy Koester with Melanie P. Brown

Photo Credit for all images: Photo by Skokie Public Library

Muslim Journeys

Grant Project Description

Troy University Libraries, in rural, southeastern Alabama hosted ten book discussions, using books from the Muslim Journeys collection developed by the National Endowment for the Humanities (NEH) for its Let's Talk About It initiative. Each library received a set of the twenty-five books. Approximately eight lectures were held with additional funding from the Alabama Humanities Foundation.

Library
Troy University Libraries
309 Wallace Hall
Troy, AL 36082

Contact
Dr. Christopher Shaffer, Dean
shafferc@troy.edu
334-670-3263

Funder
NEH (with funding as well from the Alabama Humanities Foundation)

Unusual Aspect of Grant Funding
If anything is unusual, it is that this project is funded by five grants cobbled together, although all are either directly or indirectly from the NEH or have indirect funding from the NEH.

Number of People Who Worked on Grant Application
Five library personnel and two outside faculty members were involved in writing and implementation.

Partnerships and Collaborations
We chose the Pillars of Faith theme for our first series of book discussions and partnered with a protestant church, a Jewish temple, and a mosque.

POPULATION SERVED

19,500

COLLECTION SIZE

600,000 monographs
(400,000 on main campus;
100,000 each on two
extensions)

GRANT AMOUNT

$11,011

Diverse Audiences Reached

Members of all three faiths represented by our partners attended our programming. In Dothan, we hosted primarily members of the surrounding community. On the Troy campus, we hosted large numbers of college students from a wide range of backgrounds (the Troy campus is approximately 12 percent international).

Innovative Programming Implemented

We hosted lectures by a Middle Eastern scholar from Auburn University as well as a historical fiction author who wrote a book about a brief period of harmonious relations for Muslims, Jews, and Christians that took place in Spain during the Middle Ages. For our first book discussion, we had the leaders of the three religious institutions who were partnering with us lead the discussion.

Key to Project/Proposal Success

Community partnerships with local religious organizations allowed us to reach a large number of people.

What You Would Do Differently

As the first round of book talks went on, attendance decreased. Probably, more promotion would have helped mitigate that situation. We still had double digits for all talks. This was not an issue for the second round of book talks, which had the benefit of being on a residential campus with more students being interested in the topic.

Most Difficult Part of Grant Process

We had minor criticisms from a few members (two or three) of the community, who disagreed with programs about Islam and Muslims. I was also contacted by the chief counsel for the United States Senate Budget Committee, who wanted to know why we were receiving funds from the NEH to promote the Islamic faith. I explained to him that that was not the point of the programming, or the grant, for what little that was worth.

Advice for Other Grant Seekers

Do not be discouraged if your grant application fails. Reapply, or apply to a different source.

Most Important Element of Your Success

Make sure that what you are asking for matches the goals of the grant-making agency.

Credit: Dr. Christopher Shaffer, Dean and Rachel Hooper, Business Librarian

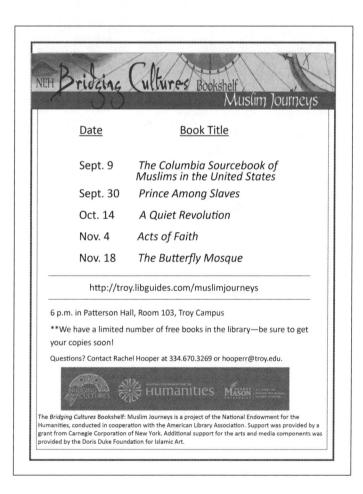

STEM 2U

Grant Project Description

The Rio Rancho Public Library STEM 2U project will make STEM (science, technology, engineering, mathematics) equipment and training available to schools and the community and build upon the public library's tradition of providing growing communities with the resources needed to learn and do new things.

Library
Rio Rancho Public Library
755 Loma Colorado Drive NE
Rio Rancho, NM 87124

Contact
Deirdre Caparoso, Youth Services Manager
dcaparoso@rrnm.gov
505-891-5013

Funder
New Mexico Library Foundation

Number of People Who Worked on Grant Application
One person, myself. I am library staff.

Partnerships and Collaborations
The Friends of the Library of Rio Rancho partnered with us as the necessary 501(c)(3) organization.

Diverse Audiences Reached
The library reached a diverse group of local educators, including homeschool families and a wide variety of public school teachers. Unlike many of our services, this particular one did target a specific group (training and equipment for educators), but we found that this group was quite diverse in its own way.

POPULATION SERVED

19,500

COLLECTION SIZE

~158,000 plus e-materials

GRANT AMOUNT

$4,587

Innovative Programming Implemented

Grant funds were used to create STEM kits that trained educators can check out. The kits feature Makey Makey, Cubelet, and littleBits components in quantities suitable for classrooms. Educators can check out kits once they have attended a short STEM kit training session.

Key to Project/Proposal Success

We were very clear on how implementation would work.

What You Would Do Differently

Probably nothing, aside from requesting additional funds. Plans have worked well.

Most Difficult Part of Grant Process

Projecting a one-year timeline more than half a year in advance—we had to be both precise and vague when doing so.

Advice for Other Grant Seekers

Again, try to be as precise and vague as you can simultaneously. This gives you a workable framework that can be adapted as need arises when implementing the grant. Overcommitting can bog you down.

Credit: Deirdre Caparoso, Youth Services Manager

Most Important Element of Your Success

A clear overall vision with easily understood objectives and goals

Every Child Ready to Read (ECRR)

Grant Project Description

Every Child Ready to Read (ECRR) programs provide parents and caregivers of young children with techniques that encourage their children to read and suggest book lists to develop prereading skills.

Library
Pueblo of Pojoaque Public Library
101 Lightning Loop
Santa Fe, NM 87506

Contact
Jill Conner, Library Director
jilcon214@gmail.com
505-455-7511

Funder
IMLS (Institute of Museum and Library Services) Enhancement Grant

Number of People Who Worked on Grant Application
One person, the library director

Partnerships and Collaborations
Partnerships were formed with the Pueblo of Pojoaque Early Childhood Center and the After-School Tutoring Program.

Diverse Audiences Reached
The project was designed for the Pueblo of Pojoaque and its tribal memberships, but the entire community, including white, African American, Asian, and Hispanic ethnic groups, benefited from programs and new materials added to the collection.

POPULATION SERVED
Legal service area of 1,907

COLLECTION SIZE
19,407 plus 1,205 e-resources

GRANT AMOUNT
$120,000

Innovative Programming Implemented

The library director and youth services librarian presented the ECRR Parent-Caregiver Workshop at other tribal libraries at their request.

Key to Project/Proposal Success

Filling a community need was the goal. Getting a grant was a method to make it happen. After six months at the Pueblo, I saw the need for regular story times and programs, especially for preschool children. I had learned about these needs in conversations with after-school tutors, local school librarians, and the young parents who were coming to the library. In getting to know the community, I heard what they most wanted at the library: more help and assistance in guiding their young children to books and a love of reading that would carry over into their first school experiences, as well as some sort of guidance on how they could encourage their children to read.

What You Would Do Differently

The process of performing all the steps outlined in the grant application was a learning process. Some worked, and some did not; we were always learning while doing and making adjustments for effectiveness.

Most Difficult Part of Grant Process

The application was a very long process because it required a complete definition, plan, budget, and timeline for delivery and review for a two-year period, but it helped me understand our needs and set them to paper in a very convincing and heartfelt manner. I had no experience writing a grant, but I had a big belief that this program was wanted and needed by the community. The grant application made the project become a reality that I was determined to have happen with that grant or another one or just somehow because it seemed so obvious.

Advice for Other Grant Seekers

Try even if you have no experience with grants. When I came to the Pueblo of Pojoaque Public Library, everyone from staff to library patrons mentioned "grants" and insisted that I should get a "grant." Never even having looked at an application, I just was not sure where to start. With patience and fortitude, I ended up sending a four-inch package of required forms and plans. Later grant reviewers commented that they felt the need and a passion that is sometimes lost in a grant proposal package.

Most Important Element of Your Success

Focusing the proposal on meeting a community need

Credit: Jill Conner, Library Director

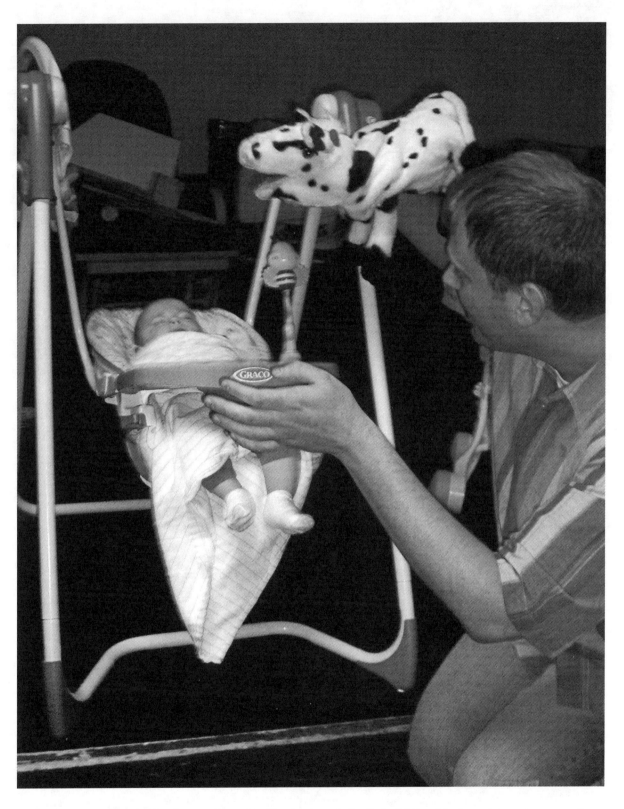

The IMLS Grant provided funding for a youth services librarian to go to the Early Childhood Center and present programs for each age group. In the Every Child Ready to Read program, no child is too young to be encouraged. Photo by Jill Conner.

Part III

Worksheets, Checklists, and Forms

Supplementary materials can be found at **www.alaeditions.org/webextras.**

Making the Commitment: A Checklist for Committing to Library Grant Work

The following questions will help you determine if your library can really make the commitment to apply for a grant.

COMMIT TO ACCOUNTABILITY

☐ Will the grant project definitely support your library's vision and mission?

☐ Will your library leadership support the project?

☐ Will the library director commit the necessary resources to the project/grant?

☐ Will the library staff have the time needed to complete the application process and to implement the project?

☐ Will the grant team have the necessary supplies, equipment, services, and space?

☐ Can the library follow through on the agreements made in the grant proposal?

☐ Will the library spend the funds as specified and keep accurate accounts?

☐ Will you make sure there are not other organizations in your community already doing your project and filling the need?

☐ Can all deadlines be met and grant reports be filed on time?

COMMIT TO EFFECTIVE COMMUNICATION

☐ Will your proposal be as clear, concise, and honest as possible?

☐ Will your goals, objectives, and activities be clearly identified and understandable?

☐ Will you be able to convey that your library and the project are important?

☐ Will you ask the funder for what you really need?

☐ Will all the library staff, board members, leadership, partners, and volunteers be continually informed about the grant?

☐ Will you ask the funder if the library's grant project clearly fits the funder's interests?

☐ Will you communicate with all your contacts?

COMMIT TO MEETING COMMUNITY NEEDS

☐ Will your library identify the needs of your community?

☐ Will your analysis include enough information to educate and inspire the funder?

☐ Can statistics be used to quantify the problems identified?

☐ Can you use stories and cases regarding specific patrons or programs to illustrate the needs?

☐ Will your grant project focus on solutions to meeting community needs?

☐ Will you identify a target audience for your grant project and involve representatives in the planning process?

COMMIT TO PLANNING

☐ Does your library have a strategic plan? Will you review it before writing your grant?

☐ Will you have a project plan that includes goals, objectives, and activities and is based on your strategic plan?

☐ Will you set deadlines?

☐ Will you organize your materials (research, grant materials, etc.)?

☐ Will you have a budgetary goal?

☐ Will you have a method to track tasks and contacts?

COMMIT TO PARTNERSHIPS

☐ Will you cultivate a strong relationship with your grant funder?

☐ Will you develop the appropriate collaborations to leverage resources, share expertise, and support the project?

☐ Will you determine what groups in your community share your library's vision and goals and approach them as partners?

☐ Will you invite community members to focus groups and planning sessions?

☐ Will you complete a partnership agreement outlining goals, responsibilities, and benefits?

COMMIT TO EVALUATION

☐ Can your library clearly identify success in respect to the grant project?

☐ Will you have an evaluation plan and/or logic model to determine if your project has met its goals?

☐ Will you be able to identify what impact your project achieves or what difference the project makes?

☐ Will you identify outcomes for the project? Will your project have meaningful results that cause a change in people's behavior, attitudes, skills, condition, or knowledge?

☐ Will you have a benchmark plan designed to measure each outcome?

COMMIT TO SUSTAINABILITY

☐ Will your project be completed?

☐ Will your project be supported by leadership after grant funds are depleted?

☐ Will you plan a funding strategy to continue your project after grant funds are depleted?

☐ Does your project involve more than just one person?

☐ If your project involves hiring new staff members, will their positions be maintained after the grant period ends?

COMMIT TO FOLLOWING THE GRANT GUIDELINES

☐ Will you check and double-check all instructions?

☐ Will you answer all questions and complete any required narrative sections?

☐ Will you compile all allowable attachments, including letters of support?

☐ Will you obtain all the required signatures?

☐ Will you submit the grant on time?

Library Planning Checklist

To compete seriously for a grant, review your library's organizational attributes periodically by considering each of the following:

☐ Does your library have a clearly defined mission statement that is the foremost consideration in all decision making?

☐ Are your goals obtainable and supportive of your library's mission?

☐ Are your objectives clear, measurable, and tied to goal achievement?

☐ Do you periodically evaluate your objectives to be certain progress is being made?

☐ Have you selected a strategy for collecting data on your community and library?

☐ Are statistics aggregated to allow for easy retrieval of necessary information?

☐ Are you recording all participants' attendance in all of your programs and projects, their feedback after their participation, and the participants' demographics?

☐ Are all statistics that are collected actually used?

☐ Are you involving library staff and community members in the planning process?

☐ Did you communicate the final plan to staff, leadership, and community members?

☐ Do you have an accurate timetable for implementation of your library's plan, and have you designated specific dates for assessing progress toward goals?

☐ Are the library's programs, services, and projects current?

☐ Have you reviewed the latest needs among the population or community that your library serves?

☐ Are all programs, services, and operations conducted in a lean but sustainable fashion?

☐ Are all unnecessary expenses cut, savings implemented, and fundraising for each program and project stepped up?

☐ Are you reporting all bookkeeping and accounting thoroughly and honestly, and does your library complete grant reports and donor requests on time and honestly?

☐ Does your library use public relations and marketing opportunities to share successes and achievements and to thank the community for its support, or does the community only hear about budget cuts and closings?

☐ Are your leadership, beneficiaries, staff, and volunteers sharing information about their work with the library, and why they've chosen to become involved with it, with their friends, colleagues, and family?

Grant Partnership Agreement Worksheet

To be completed by the library and each individual partner.

Library Name and Contact Information: _____
_____
_____
_____

Partner(s) Name and Contact Information: _____
_____
_____
_____

Project Name: _____
_____

Overview of Project (project description, goals, objectives, activities, and project outcomes): _____
_____
_____
_____

Goals of This Partnership: _____
_____
_____
_____

Resources to Be Provided (staff, funding, equipment, facilities, and which partner will provide): _____
_____
_____
_____

Services to Be Provided (include programs, services, and activities and party responsible): _____
_____
_____
_____

Project Timeline (include period of partnership, progress review dates, activities, etc.): _____
_____
_____
_____

Implementation Plan (outline all roles and responsibilities regarding this partnership): _____
_____
_____
_____

Impact of Partnership on Each Partner (gains and losses, including any products to be
created or resources purchased with grant funds or shared funds): _____
_____
_____
_____

Sustainability Plans: _____
_____
_____
_____

Evaluation Process (include required reports along with due dates and party responsible): _____
_____
_____
_____

**We agree to the validity of all of the above statements and agree to fulfill the obligations specified.
We further agree to each of the following:**

- ☐ To implement the project as presented in the grant application
- ☐ To use funds or services received in accordance with the grant application and any applicable laws and
regulations
- ☐ To maintain honest communications with the partnering agency

Signatures: _____
_____
_____

Today's Date: _____

Strategic Plan Worksheet

GOALS FROM STRATEGIC PLAN	OBJECTIVES FROM STRATEGIC PLAN	ACTIVITIES FROM STRATEGIC PLAN
Goal 1	Objective 1.1	1 _____
		2 _____
		3 _____
		4 _____
		5 _____
	Objective 1.2	1 _____
		2 _____
		3 _____
		4 _____
		5 _____
	Objective 1.3	1 _____
		2 _____
		3 _____
		4 _____
		5 _____

GOALS FROM STRATEGIC PLAN	OBJECTIVES FROM STRATEGIC PLAN	ACTIVITIES FROM STRATEGIC PLAN
Goal 2	Objective 2.1	1
		2
		3
		4
		5
	Objective 2.2	1
		2
		3
		4
		5
	Objective 2.3	1
		2
		3
		4
		5

GOALS FROM STRATEGIC PLAN	OBJECTIVES FROM STRATEGIC PLAN	ACTIVITIES FROM STRATEGIC PLAN
Goal 3	Objective 3.1	1 _____
		2 _____
		3 _____
		4 _____
		5 _____
	Objective 3.2	1 _____
		2 _____
		3 _____
		4 _____
		5 _____
	Objective 3.3	1 _____
		2 _____
		3 _____
		4 _____
		5 _____

GOALS FROM STRATEGIC PLAN	OBJECTIVES FROM STRATEGIC PLAN	ACTIVITIES FROM STRATEGIC PLAN	
Goal 4	Objective 4.1	1	
		2	
		3	
		4	
		5	
	Objective 4.2	1	
		2	
		3	
		4	
		5	
	Objective 4.3	1	
		2	
		3	
		4	
		5	

Project Planning Worksheet

1. Project Description

Briefly describe your project. Include why you are doing this project, who will benefit, what you will do, where it will take place, and with whom.

_____
_____
_____
_____

2. Keywords

List the keywords that describe your project.

_____
_____
_____

3. Needs Statement

Describe the need in your community or the problem your project will address.

_____
_____
_____

4. Target Audience

Describe the target audience for the project.

_____
_____
_____

5. Project Goals

List the goals of the project.

_____
_____
_____
_____

6. Project Outcomes

Describe how the project will impact a community problem and list the outcomes for people in terms of what knowledge they will gain, what skills they will learn, which behaviors will change, how their quality of life will improve, and so forth.

_____

_____

_____

7. Project Objectives

List SMART (specific, measurable, achievable, realistic, and time-bound) objectives for the project.
Explain how you will know when you have solved this problem.

_____

_____

_____

8. Project Action Steps

List the steps or activities required to make the changes listed above. Develop strategies to reach the objectives.

_____

_____

_____

9. Resources Needed

List the resources you will need to accomplish the steps. Note the resources you already have.

_____

_____

_____

10. Partners and Collaborators

List your potential partners. Note who else is likely to help you address this problem in your community.

_____

_____

_____

11. Project Budget

Detail how much this project will cost to implement.

_____

_____

_____

12. Evaluation

Describe how you will measure your success to show that you have reached your objectives.

_____

_____

_____

_____

Project Action Steps Worksheet

PROJECT OBJECTIVES	PERSONNEL	ACTION STEPS
1		
2		
3		

Project Timeline Worksheet

ACTIVITY	PERSONNEL	MONTH											
		1	2	3	4	5	6	7	8	9	10	11	12

Personnel Budget Worksheet

POSITION	SALARY	BENEFITS (___%)	TOTAL

TOTAL PERSONNEL COSTS

Nonpersonnel Budget Worksheet

ITEM	DESCRIPTION	COST
Marketing		
Equipment		
Copying Costs		
Supplies		
Space Rental		
Travel		
Other		

TOTAL NONPERSONNEL COSTS

Project Budget Worksheet

PERSONNEL BUDGET

Position	Total Cost	Match	$ Requested
Total Personnel Costs			

NONPERSONNEL BUDGET

Item	Total Cost	Match	$ Requested
Total Nonpersonnel Costs			

TOTAL PROJECT COSTS

Evaluation Plan Worksheet

GOAL	OUTCOME	OBJECTIVE	EVALUATION METHOD	TIMELINE

Keyword Selection Worksheet

PROJECT PLAN	KEYWORDS
Goals	
1.	
2.	
3.	
Outcomes	
1.	
2.	
3.	
Objectives	
1.	
2.	
3.	
Activities and Action Steps	
1.	
2.	
3.	
4.	
5.	
6.	
7.	
8.	
9.	
10.	

Funder Summary Worksheet

Use this form to record information about funders that are possible matches for your grant project.

Funder Name: _____

Address: _____

Contact Person: _____

Funder's Financial Information

Funding awarded last year: _____

Number of grants awarded: _____

Average amount awarded: _____

Funder's Interests and Criteria

Funder's purpose/mission: _____

Fields/topics of interest: _____

Eligibility criteria: _____

Geographic area served: _____

Application Information

Approach (letter of interest, proposal, etc.): _____

Application form: ☐ Yes ☐ No   Where found/format: _____

Deadlines: _____

Sources Used

Where did you find the information about this funder? (list websites, directories, etc.): _____

_____

_____

_____

990 IRS form: _____

Annual report: _____

Personal contacts: _____

Notes: _____

_____

_____

_____

_____

Winning Grants Sources and Resources Handout

Government Grants

Grants.gov, http://grants.gov

The access point for over 1,000 grant programs totaling $400 billion in awards offered by the twenty-six federal grant-making agencies.

Top Government Funders for Libraries

Federal
- Institute of Museum and Library Services, www.imls.gov
- U.S. Department of Education, www2.ed.gov/fund/grants-apply.html
- National Library of Medicine, www.nlm.nih.gov/grants.html
- National Endowment for the Arts, www.nea.gov/grants
- National Endowment for the Humanities, www.neh.gov/grants/index.html
- National Archives, www.archives.gov/nhprc/announcement

State
- Your State Humanities Council, www.neh.gov/about/state-humanities-councils
- Your State Arts Council, www.nasaa-arts.org/About/State-Arts-Agency-Directory
- Your State Department of Education, www2.ed.gov/about/contacts/state/index.html
- Your State Library, www.imls.gov/grants/grants-state/state-profiles

Local

- Your City/County Government, www.statelocalgov.net (Contact your local departments of arts, business, community development, environment, historical preservation, education, youth, technology, and archives.)

Private Grants Foundations

- The Foundation Center, http://foundationcenter.org, is the largest and most comprehensive resource for researching foundations. Includes many resources for researching foundations, discovering trends in grant making, and finding top foundations in your geographic region.

  - Websites of Private Foundations, http://foundationcenter.org/findfunders/foundfinder
  - RFP Bulletin, http://philanthropynewsdigest.org/rfps
  - Foundation Center Funding Information Networks, http://foundationcenter.org/ask-us/funding-information-network, located throughout the United States, mostly in libraries. Lots of books and databases!

- Community Foundations have resource materials, local directories, and more information about funding opportunities in your area. Use the Council on Foundation's Community Foundation Locator, www.cof.org/community-foundation-locator.

Corporations

Visit websites of corporations that operate in your community for information about their priorities, grant guidelines, and deadlines. Target, Dollar General, Best Buy, Walmart, and Barnes & Noble all have giving programs. The National Directory of Corporate Giving is a helpful print directory from the Foundation Center.

Professional Library Associations

Many grants and awards for library projects and personnel.
- ALA's "Awards, Grants and Scholarships," www.ala.org/ala/awardsgrants
- "PLA Awards and Grants," www.ala.org/pla/awards
- Your state library association, www.ala.org/groups/affiliates/chapters/state/stateregional

Local Sources

- The Grantsmanship Center, www.tgci.com/funding/states.asp, maintains information about your state's foundations, community foundations, corporate giving programs, and the top forty foundations in your state.
- Local Clubs and Organizations with giving programs: Research listed organizations in your local community directories (including the Yellow Pages), visit Michigan State University's list of service clubs and civic organizations (http://staff.lib.msu.edu/harris23/grants/servicec.htm), and ask library Friends, board members, and staff for ideas.
- Local Businesses: Inquire with banks, grocery stores, insurance companies, drugstores, etc.

Print Resources

- *Winning Grants: A How-To-Do-It Manual for Librarians*, by Stephanie Gerding and Pamela H. MacKellar (ALA Editions, 2016).
- *The ALA Book of Library Grant Money*, edited by Nancy Kalikow Maxwell, with profiles of private and corporate foundations and direct corporate givers receptive to library grant proposals (ALA Editions, 2014).
- *Annual Register of Grant Support* (Information Today, annual), a print directory that lists grants from both government and private sources.

Blogs, Newsletters, and Bulletins

- Library Grants blog, http://librarygrants.blogspot.com, a free website of library grant opportunities maintained by librarians Gerding and MacKellar
- Primary Source, www.imls.gov/news/primary_source.aspx, the Institute of Museum and Library Services' monthly e-mail newsletter
- Foundation Center Training, http://grantspace.org/training
- Grants.gov grant opportunity e-mails, www.grants.gov/web/grants/manage-subscriptions.html
- Association of Fundraising Professionals, www.afpnet.org
- The Grantsmanship Center, www.tgci.com/training/tprogram.asp
- Chronicle of Philanthropy, www.philanthropy.com

Statistical Sources

- U.S. Census Bureau's American Fact Finder, http://factfinder.census.gov/faces/nav/jsf/pages/index.xhtml
- Digital Inclusion Survey Interactive Map, http://digitalinclusion.umd.edu/content/interactive-map
- IMLS, Find Your Library, www.imls.gov/research-evaluation/data-collection/public-libraries-survey/find-your-library
- IMLS, Explore PLS Data, www.imls.gov/research-evaluation/data-collection/public-libraries-survey/explore-pls-data
- The Annie E. Casey Foundation, Kids Count Data Center, http://datacenter.kidscount.org
- Library Research Services, www.lrs.org/data-tools
- ALA: Research and Statistics, www.ala.org/research
- USA.gov, State, Local, and Tribal Governments, www.usa.gov/state-tribal-governments

Questions for Funders Checklist

☐ Is my library eligible for your grants?

☐ How are applications reviewed?

☐ Are specific screening criteria or a rubric used? May we have a copy?

☐ May we submit a draft of the grant proposal for review before the final deadline?

☐ If I briefly describe the project, would you provide suggestions or advice?

☐ Are copies of successful grant proposals available?

☐ May we include our strategic plan or other supporting documentation in an appendix?

☐ May we include a table of contents?

☐ How and when are final decisions made?

☐ Will we be notified that our grant proposal has been received?

Grant Proposal Worksheet

Library Name: _____

Library Address: _____

Library Address2: _____

Library Telephone Number: _____

Date: _____

Grant Proposal submitted to (*Name of Prospective Funder*): _____

GRANT PROJECT TITLE:

Date: _____

Name, Title (*Funder Contact Person*): _____

Funder Name (*Foundation, Government Agency, etc.*): _____

Funder Address: _____

Funder Address2: _____

RE: Title of Grant: _____

Dear Name of Funder Contact: _____

◇◇◇◇◇◇◇◇◇◇◇◇◇◇◇◇◇

Name of Library is pleased to submit this proposal for your review. We look forward to your partnership in our efforts to serve *Name of Your Community*.

Our much-needed project, *Title of Project*, is a partnership among *Insert Name of Library and project partners. Insert the one-sentence project description from your Project Planning Worksheet.*

Insert the needs statement from your Project Planning Worksheet. Insert the project goals from your Project Planning Worksheet.

The Name of Library is committed to the success of this project. *Insert a statement of any outside funding that will be used toward the project.* Our request to Name of Funder is for Total Amount of Funding Requested. *Insert a statement regarding planning accomplished and/or involvement of target audience.*

Insert your library mission and a sentence or two from your organizational overview. Particularly demonstrate why the library is a viable grant candidate.

Thank you for your time and attention. We look forward to working together to build a better community. Please do not hesitate to contact us with any questions or requests for additional information.

Sincerely,
Name of Library Director or Other Authority
Title of Library Director or Other Authority

Table of Contents

Proposal Summary

Date of Application:
Name of Library (exact legal name):
Library's Full Mailing Address:

Library Director: *Library Director's Full Name; Library Director's Contact Information*
Grant Coordinator: *Grant Coordinator's Name, if not Director; include title Grant Coordinator's Contact Information*
Project Title: *Project Title*
Project Description: *Insert one-sentence project description from Project Planning Worksheet*
Amount Requested: *$$*
Project Funding from Other Sources: *$$; include in-kind contributions from library, other grant funds*
Total Project Budget: *$$*
Project Budget Time Period: *Dates covered by project budget (June 1, 20XX–May 31, 20XX)*
Grant Abstract: *In 500 or fewer words, condense the major points of each of the grant proposal components. You will want to write this section last and definitely review it as the last step in editing your proposal.*

Include:
- A few sentences summarizing the library's organizational overview, which will show why the library is the best choice for implementing the grant project
- Any partners, and how they are contributing

- The needs statement, as well as the target audience
- A few sentences from the project description detailing what the project entails and how it fulfills the needs
- The project goals, objectives, and/or outcomes
- A brief overview of the evaluation methods to be used
- How the funder's mission aligns with your grant project

Organizational Overview

Include a brief overview of the library's history, mission, qualifications, trustworthiness, community served, achievements and impact in community, primary programs, and current budget. Provde a sentence or two detailing the qualifications of key staff and library leadership/board. Include brief success stories if relevant to the project and funder.

Statement of Needs

Establish the existence and importance of the problem. This is a critical part of your proposal. A compelling needs statement will motivate the funder to assist in the solution. Prove that the need is relevant to the funder. Why should the funder fund this project, why now, and how will it benefit the library community?

The need should focus on those your library serves, not just the library. Support the need with evidence (research from statistics, experts, or census data; or information from the library's long-range plan, such as the community analysis or needs assessments). You may even include anecdotal substantiation, such as a personal story of someone who needs this project or input from focus groups.

Then prove why the library has the ability to respond to the need you have identified. Link the fulfillment of the need to your library's mission.

Answer the questions:
- Why this issue?
- Why this target population?
- Why this funder?
- Why your library?

Project Description

This section includes an overview of your project. It is a more in-depth narrative than the project abstract. In the previous section, you discussed the needs; now you will focus on the solutions. Briefly summarize the project and how it will be of benefit to the target population. Include the project goals, project objectives, and project partners. You may also include information on how the project will be sustained after the initial funding.

Include:
- Project significance (*include one or two sentences developed from the needs statement*)
- Target audience
- Project goals
- Project objectives
- Project partners
- Plans for sustainability and leveraging impact

Approach/Methodology

How and when will the project be implemented? Describe the strategies and methods to be used and why they are the most effective solution to the need. Include project action steps and emphasize project partners and collaborators. Include a timeline (example follows). Mention how the donor will be recognized.

ACTIVITY List each grant activity in this column.	JAN	FEB	MAR	APR	MAY	JUNE	JULY	AUG	SEPT	OCT	NOV	DEC

Budget Request

Personnel

POSITION	SALARY	BENEFITS (%)	TOTAL
Example: .20 FTE Library Assistant	$	$	$
Example: .15 FTE Reference Librarian	$	$	$
Complete according to Budget Template.	$	$	$
	$	$	$
Total Personnel Costs	$	$	$

Nonpersonnel

CATEGORIES	TOTAL AMOUNT	AMOUNT FUNDED	AMOUNT REQUESTED
Marketing			
Insert any subcategories (brochures, ads, etc.)	$	$	$
Equipment			
Technology			

Budget Request

Nonpersonnel (continued)

CATEGORIES	TOTAL AMOUNT	AMOUNT FUNDED	AMOUNT REQUESTED
Supplies			
Postage Delivery			
Printing and Copying			
TOTAL NONPERSONNEL COSTS	$	$	$
TOTAL PERSONNEL COSTS	$	$	$
TOTAL PROJECT BUDGET	$	$	$

Evaluation Process

Provide a brief description of the evaluation plan for judging the success of the project. How will you measure success? How will you use the results? What reports will the donor receive and when?

GOAL	OUTCOME	OBJECTIVE	EVALUATION METHOD	TIME PERIOD
1. Complete according to Project Evaluation Plan Template.	Complete according to Project Evaluation Plan Template.	Complete according to Project Evaluation Plan Template.	Complete according to Project Evaluation Plan Template.	Complete according to Project Evaluation Plan Template.
2.				
3.				
4.				

Appendix

Some funders specify what should and should not be included in the appendix. If this is not specified in the grant guidelines, contact the funder to verify anything you wish to include that is not approved. Some examples of appendix materials include strategic plans, résumés or job descriptions of key personnel, organizational charts, letters of support, financial reports, the budget for the current year, lengthy charts and tables, IRS 501(c)(3) nonprofit determination letter, a recent library newsletter, or relevant newspaper clippings that demonstrate the library's applicable work.

Grant Submission Checklist

☐ The funder is interested in receiving my proposal.

☐ This proposal reflects the funder's areas of interest.

☐ We have followed the instructions and guidelines of the funder's specifications.

☐ Our proposal meets the page/word limits.

☐ The font type and size are correct.

☐ The margin size is correct.

☐ The line spacing is correct.

☐ We have used the specified type of paper, if indicated.

☐ We did not bind the proposal unless we were told we could.

☐ We sent the correct number of copies and the original; we also retained a copy for ourselves and copies were made for partners and supporters.

☐ We included letters of support.

☐ We have the required signatures.

☐ The proposal components are titled and compiled in the order specified.

- Title sheet
- Cover letter
- Table of contents
- Proposal summary
- Organizational overview
- Statement of needs
- Project description
- Timeline
- Budget request
- Evaluation process
- Appendix

☐ The cover letter explains the project and states the total cost of the project, the amount expected from other sources, and the amount requested.

☐ The project description specifies the need that will be met and how people will benefit.

☐ The project description tells the whole story of our project in clear, understandable language.

☐ The objectives are measurable.

☐ The methodology explains how the objectives will be met.

☐ The timeline includes all major activities and who will do them.

☐ The evaluation plan measures the degree to which the objectives and outcomes are met.

☐ The project includes partners and reflects community involvement.

☐ The budget is reasonable and the calculations are correct.

☐ The project is sustainable.

☐ Adequate personnel are identified in the proposal to do the project.

☐ Adequate resources are available to do the project.

☐ Our library has the capacity to do the project.

☐ The proposal contains no jargon or acronyms.

☐ If attachments are included, we have confirmed that the funder allows them.

☐ The proposal has been proofread by an impartial person.

☐ The proposal is clear and easy to understand by someone outside the grant team.

☐ Letters of agreement from partners and letters of support from supporters are included, if allowed.

☐ We have met the deadline.

☐ The proposal looks professional.

Now, carefully go through your application with your checklist and check off every item as you make sure it is in place. Once everything is checked, you may seal the envelope and head for the post office.

☐ The proposal was submitted on _____.

☐ We have a dated receipt or confirmation that the proposal was submitted.

Debrief and Review Checklist

☐ Did we remain true to the strategic plan?

☐ Was our project designed to meet community needs?

☐ Did we work well as a team?

☐ Where did we excel as a team? Where could we improve?

☐ Did we delegate well?

☐ Is there anything we overlooked?

☐ What would we do differently?

☐ Did we forget to include a potential partner?

☐ Did we complete everything on time?

☐ Did we feel rushed getting authorized signatures, submitting the proposal before the deadline, getting proper approvals, or gathering letters of support?

☐ Was it stressful? How could we reduce the stress next time?

☐ If we were successful this time, why were we successful?

☐ If we were unsuccessful this time, why were we unsuccessful? What were the funder's comments about our proposal and how can we improve?

Glossary

501(c)(3): A provision of the U.S. federal tax code that designates a nonprofit organization be exempt from some federal income taxes. Organizations described in 501(c)(3) are commonly referred to as charitable organizations or public charities and may have goals that are literary, religious, educational, or scientific. Some funders may require proof of this type of nonprofit status with an application.

990-PF: The federal reporting form that private grant-making foundations are required to submit every year to the Internal Revenue Service (IRS). 990-PFs document a foundation's financial activities during the year. These are public documents, and the information in them may be used to learn about a foundation, its trustees, where its funds originate, its grant-making contributions, and to whom it has previously awarded grants.

abstract: Usually a one-page summary of a grant project, including all pertinent activities, a summary of the objectives, and the expected results.

action steps: The specific steps taken to accomplish a grant project.

activities: The specific actions or strategies that will accomplish the long-range or strategic plan.

annual report: A report published yearly by a foundation or corporation describing its activities, including grants awarded. Annual reports may be simple or very elaborate. Annual reports may be used as a way to inform the community about contributions, programs, and activities. Annual reports may also serve as marketing tools.

appendixes/attachments: Supporting documentation that is submitted with a proposal. Requirements vary, so be sure to check the application guidelines carefully for what the funder will accept. See pages 116–117 in chapter 6 for more details.

application: The formal documents that are submitted to a potential funder when seeking funds.

audit, financial: An examination of an organization's financial documents by an outside expert. Financial audits are usually conducted at the end of the fiscal year. The funder may require an audit of grant funds at the end of a project.

audit, program: A review of the activities and results of a funded program by the funding agency. A program audit may be mandatory or random, at the end of a project or midstream. Also known as monitoring.

authorized signature: The official signature of the person who is responsible for an organization by law.

beneficiary: A member of the target population whom the grant benefits. For example, a community member attending a library program is the beneficiary of a grant received by the library.

bricks and mortar: Generally refers to capital funds used for building renovation or construction.

budget: An annual fiscal plan for an organization that contains an itemized list of revenues and expenses. The library's annual budget may be included in the grant proposal appendix. A project budget is often included in a grant proposal and covers estimated funds needed for the entire grant project.

capital/building grant: Funds that are used to purchase land and construct, renovate, or expand buildings and facilities. May also refer to major equipment purchases, such as computer networks.

challenge grant: A grant that requires the grantee to generate additional funds from other sources, usually within a specified period.

community committee: A committee whose members include those served by the library and who often serve as advisors to strategic or project planning. These members may include representatives from local leadership, business, government, parents, students, and all parts of the library community.

community foundation: A tax-exempt, nonprofit philanthropic organization comprised of funds established by many donors for the charitable benefit of the residents in a defined geographic area or community.

cooperating collection library: A member of the Foundation Center's network of libraries, community foundations, and other nonprofit agencies that provides a core collection of Foundation Center publications in addition to a variety of additional materials and services in areas useful to grant seekers.

corporate foundation: A private foundation that amasses its grant funds from the contributions of a profit-making corporation. The corporate foundation is a legally separate organization from the parent corporation. Corporate foundations are subject to the rules and regulations that oversee all private foundations.

corporate giving program: A grant-making program established and administered within a for-profit corporation. Some companies make grants through both a corporate giving program and a corporate foundation.

demonstration grant: A grant made to implement an innovative project or program. If successful, this kind of grant may serve as a model, to be duplicated by others.

discretionary grant: The category of federal or state grants for which individual libraries, community organizations, schools, and local governments are eligible to apply. Unlike the federal grant funds that are distributed through a pass-through agent, such as the state.

donated products: Any goods, products, equipment, or other tangible property that is donated to a library for its use and ownership. These may include food, paper goods, or office supplies as well as furnishings, computer equipment, vehicles, and so forth. Donated products may be considered part of "in-kind" support and can be included in a budget at fair-market value.

drawdown: The method by which a grantee requests payment from the funding agency. Frequency of drawdowns (or draws) may be weekly, quarterly, or a single lump sum payment at the end of the project.

DUNS number: A unique nine-digit number issued by Dun and Bradstreet that is used to keep track of more than 70 million businesses worldwide. The federal government requires organizations to provide a DUNS number in federal grant applications and proposals.

EIN (employer identification number): This number is issued by the Internal Revenue Service (IRS) and must be included in all government and some foundation grant applications.

evaluation plan: An evaluation plan includes the methods used to examine, monitor, and determine the effectiveness and results of a project or activity. Evaluation aids in determining grant achievements, outputs, and outcomes and communicating those results to the funders and to the community. Different types of evaluation plans include outcome-based evaluation, quantitative evaluation, formative evaluation, and summative evaluation. (See chapter 3.)

fiscal year (FY): A twelve-month accounting period that includes the period covered by an annual budget. It does not necessarily coincide with the calendar year; some fiscal years begin on July 1, others on October 1.

focus group: A group of individuals gathered together to discuss an issue or give feedback. Focus groups may be used to determine the library community's needs or to plan or evaluate a grant project.

formula grants: Grants from the federal or state government to a lower level of government for which a specific monetary amount is determined based on a formula, usually derived from socioeconomic data and usually noncompetitive.

foundation: A nonprofit organization with its own funds/endowments that is managed by its own trustees/directors and usually benefits educational, charitable, social, religious, or other activities. Types of foundations include community foundations, corporate foundations, family foundations, and private foundations.

funder: The agency, organization, foundation, association, or government unit that awards grants. Also known as a funding agency, grant maker, grantor, or donor.

funding cycle: The schedule of events that starts with the announcement of the availability of funds and is followed by the deadline for submission of applications, submission of applications, review of applications, grant awards, contract documents, and release of funds.

goal: The broad purpose of a project or program; the result the project or program is attempting to achieve.

grant: The sum of money given to support the project or program of an agency, organization, or individual. This is usually the result of a formal proposal submission and review process. Grants are given with no conditions for repayment.

grant agreement: A contract entered into by the recipient of a grant and a funder. Based on the application submitted, the agreement commits the recipient to implement a specific project, within a certain time frame, for a specific amount of money.

grant coordinator: The individual responsible for all activities involved in the grant, including planning, submission, evaluation, implementation, and follow-up.

grant proposal components: The standard sections of a grant proposal. These will vary according to each funder. Typical components include these: title sheet, cover letter, table of contents, proposal summary, organizational overview, statement of needs, project description, approach/methodology, budget, evaluation plan, and appendix.

grant team: This team is comprised of representatives from library leadership, community advisors, grant researchers, grant writers, subject matter experts, and staff members who will plan and implement the grant.

grantee: The recipient of grant funds. May also be referred to as fundee or donee.

guidelines: A funder's goals, priorities, criteria, and procedures for applying for a grant.

IMLS (Institute of Museum and Library Services): A federal grant-making agency that promotes leadership, innovation, and a lifetime of learning by supporting museums and libraries in the United States. Created by the Museum and Library Services Act of 1996 (www.imls.gov).

indirect cost: This represents the cost of doing business that is not readily identified with a particular grant project but is necessary for the general operation of the organization. This may include heat, light, rent, accounting, and other supporting administrative costs.

in-kind support: A noncash donation of labor, facilities, or equipment to carry out a project. Examples are products or equipment, volunteer services, office space or staff time, and library materials—donated for a project. In-kind support should always be included in a budget at fair-market value.

lead agency: The organization with the primary responsibility for overseeing the grant project, including filing reports and fiscal management.

letter of inquiry: A brief letter to assess a potential funder's interest in considering a grant proposal. It should include background on the library; a brief description of the project; the total amount required to fund the project; the specific dollar amount requested from the funder; the amount on hand from other sources; and an explanation of why the proposal matches the funder's priorities and interests. If interested, the funder will invite submission of a full proposal.

letter of intent: A letter that the grant seeker sends before writing or submitting a grant proposal to a funder to ensure that the proposal will fit within the funder's guidelines and mission. Funders may identify possible organizations they are interested in funding and request a letter of intent.

letter of support: A simple letter of endorsement or commitment to the grant project submitted with a proposal. This letter should be from project experts, supporters, partners, or collaborators who explain why they believe the project should be funded.

library service responses: Library service responses were created by the Public Library Association (PLA) and are used in the planning process in *Strategic Planning for Results* by Sandra S. Nelson (2008). They are used to prioritize the activities most needed by the library's community. See the list on page 23.

LSTA (Library Services and Technology Act): A section of the Museum and Library Services Act passed in 1996, it provides funds to state library agencies using a population-based formula. State libraries may use the appropriation to support statewide initiatives and services; they may also distribute the funds through competitive subgrant competitions or cooperative agreements to public, academic, research, school, and special libraries in their state.

matching funds: In some grants, the portion of the project costs that the grantee is responsible for providing. Examples of matching funds are funding from other sources, personnel, or in-kind donations.

mission: A broad statement of the role or purpose of the library, whom the library serves, and justification of its existence.

narrative: The written portion of a grant. The story of the grant project's who, what, where, when, why, and how.

needs assessment: A method of collecting information to determine how well the library is serving its community and what other services or resources it can provide in the future.

needs statement: The part of the grant in which it is explained, using both qualitative and quantitative data, the problem or opportunity addressed by the grant project or program and why the library should be funded.

nonprofit: A group that exists for reasons such as serving a public good, rather than to make a profit, such as charitable, educational, religious, or service organizations.

objectives: The desired outcomes of activities or success indicators. Objectives specify who, what, when, and how the criteria by which the effectiveness of a project will be measured. Objectives should be specific, measurable, achievable, realistic, and time-bound (SMART).

operating expenses: Expenses that include all the costs of keeping a library open, including salaries, utilities, maintenance, insurance, accounting expenses, and so forth. These are the expenses of internal and administrative operations, rather than costs for specific programs or services.

outcome-based evaluation (OBE): Sometimes called outcomes measurement, this is a systematic way to determine if a program has achieved its goals. Many government agencies require that OBE be integrated into grant projects to measure meaningful results that change people's attitudes, skills, knowledge, behavior, or life condition.

outcomes: Expected results of a project that can be used to measure its success.

partner: Another organization that is sharing responsibility with a library for a grant project or specific goals. Some funders require partners to be involved in grant projects.

partnership agreement: A statement or letter from partners stating that they agree to collaborate on a particular grant project, specifying their obligations and contributions to the project. This may take the form of an MOU (memorandum of understanding).

PI (principal investigator): Someone in charge of directing the grant project or activities being supported by the grant.

pre-award office: An office within the grants and contracts office in most university settings that searches for grant opportunities, assists with developing proposals, coordinates grant seeking across university departments, reviews proposals, coordinates required signatures, and approves proposals before submission.

program officer: A staff member of a funding agency who reviews grant proposals, processes applications, and knows the ins and outs of the funder's interests, guidelines, and application procedures.

project director: The individual responsible for activities involved in the grant project, including implementation, evaluation, and follow-up.

project grant: Funds given to support a specific, well-defined project or set of activities designed to address a specific need or achieve a specific goal.

project team: Representatives from library leadership, community advisors, grant researchers, grant writers, staff members, and subject matter experts who will plan and implement the grant project.

proposal: A written or electronic application submitted to a government agency, foundation, or corporation to request a grant. Requirements vary widely among funders regarding contents, length, format, and accompanying materials.

request for proposal (RFP): The formal announcement issued by a grant maker declaring that it is seeking proposals for funding in specific topic or program areas. The RFP usually includes complete details on the kinds of services or programs the grant maker will consider; proposal guidelines; deadline; proposal review and evaluation criteria; and other information to help in preparing a proposal.

research grant: A grant made to support a specific project that has a primary purpose of inquiry or examination into facts, studies, or investigations. The result may be a detailed paper with recommendations for future plans.

seed money: Funding to support a new project in its start-up stage. Sometimes seed money will be granted to begin a new program in its infancy until a larger funding source is found. Also known as start-up money.

site visit: A visit made by the funder to the grantee at the location of the project or program. The purpose is to meet with staff and beneficiaries to observe and sometimes evaluate the project in action.

state library: The official agencies charged with statewide library development and the administration of federal funds authorized by the Library Services and Technology Act (LSTA). These agencies vary greatly, are located in various departments of state government, and report to different authorities depending on the state. They are involved in various ways in the leadership of enhancing library service for all the residents of the state.

sustainability: Refers to an organization's ability to keep a grant project going after the initial funding has been used.

target population: The people who will benefit from the project the grant is funding, such as teens, the unemployed, or computer users.

timeline: A systematic method of planning activities that will be implemented, arranged by date or time. This may be the beginning, implementation, and end of each grant activity displayed in a chart or narrative format in a month-by-month time frame.

Bibliography

Association of Fundraising Professionals. www.afpnet.org/index.cfm.

Bailey, Lanie, and Beverly A. Browning. *Winning Strategies for Developing Grant Proposals.* Washington, DC: Thompson, 2007.

Bauer, David G. *How to Evaluate and Improve Your Grants Effort.* Westport, CT: American Council on Education/Oryx Press, 2001.

———. *The "How To" Grants Manual: Successful Grantseeking Techniques for Obtaining Public and Private Grants.* 8th ed. Lanham, MD: Rowman and Littlefield, 2015.

Brown, Larissa Golden, Martin John Brown, and Judith E. Nichols. *Demystifying Grant Seeking: What You Really Need to Do to Get the Grants.* New York: Wiley, 2001.

Browning, Beverly A. *Grant Writing for Dummies.* 5th ed. Hoboken, NJ: J. Wiley and Sons, 2014.

———. *Perfect Phrases for Writing Grant Proposals: Hundreds of Ready-to-Use Phrases to Present Your Organization, Explain Your Cause, and Get the Funding You Need.* New York: McGraw-Hill, 2008.

———. *Winning Strategies for Developing Grant Proposals.* Washington, DC: Thompson Publications, 2006.

Bryson, John. *Strategic Planning for Public and Nonprofit Organizations: A Guide to Strengthening and Sustaining Organizational Achievement.* 4th ed. San Francisco: Jossey-Bass, 2011.

Burke, J. *I'll Grant You That: A Step-by-Step Guide to Finding Funds, Designing Winning Projects, and Writing Powerful Grant Proposals.* Portsmouth, NH: Heinemann, 2000.

Bushe, Gervase R. *Clear Leadership: Sustaining Real Collaboration and Partnership at Work.* Rev. ed. Boston, MA: Davies-Black Publishers, 2010.

Carlson, Mim. *Winning Grants Step by Step: The Complete Workbook for Planning, Developing, and Writing Successful Proposals.* 4th ed. Jossey-Bass Nonprofit and Public Management Series. San Francisco: Jossey-Bass, 2013.

Catalog of Federal Domestic Assistance (CFDA). www.cfda.gov.

Chronicle of Philanthropy, The. https://philanthropy.com.

Clarke, Cheryl A. *Storytelling for Grantseekers: The Guide to Creative Nonprofit Fundraising.* San Francisco: Jossey-Bass, 2002.

Corporate Philanthropy Report. San Francisco, CA: John Wiley and Sons, monthly.

Council on Foundations. www.cof.org.

Disability.gov. "Disability.gov's Guide to Federal Government Grants." www.disability.gov/resource/disability-govs-guide-to-federal-government-grants.

Federal Register: The Daily Journal of the United States Government. www.federalregister.gov.

Florida Department of State, Division of Library and Information Services. *Workbook: Outcome Measurement of Library Programs.* Tallahassee, FL: Florida Department of State, 2000. dlis.dos.state.fl.us/bld/Research_Office/OutcomeEvalWkbk.doc.

Forsberg, Kevin, Hal Mooz, and Howard Cotterman. *Visualizing Project Management: Models and Frameworks for Mastering Complex Systems.* 3rd ed. Hoboken, NJ: Wiley and Sons, 2005.

Foundation Center. http://foundationcenter.org.

———. "990 Finder." http://foundationcenter.org/find-funding/990-finder.

———. *Foundation Directory Online* and FDO Quick Start. https://fdo.foundationcenter.org.

———. *Grants for Arts, Culture and the Humanities.* Digital ed. New York: Foundation Center, 2015.

———. *Grants for Capacity Building, Management and Technical Assistance.* Digital ed. New York: Foundation Center, 2015.

———. *Grants for Children and Youth.* Digital ed. New York: Foundation Center, 2015.

———. *Grants for People with Disabilities.* Digital ed. New York: Foundation Center, 2015.

———. *Grants for the Aging.* Digital ed. New York: Foundation Center, 2015.

———. "Introduction to Finding Grants Webinar." http://grantspace.org/training/self-paced -training/introduction-to-finding-grants.

———. "Introduction to Proposal Writing Webinar." http://grantspace.org/training/ self-paced-training/introduction-to-proposal-writing-webinar.

———. *National Directory of Corporate Giving.* 19th ed. New York: Foundation Center, 2013.

Fundsnet Services. www.fundsnetservices.com.

Geever, Jane C. *The Foundation Center's Guide to Proposal Writing.* 6th ed. New York: Foundation Center, 2012.

Gerding, Stephanie R. "Small Library, Big Fundraising: Community Support Is Way Above Par." *Computers in Libraries* 23, no. 2 (February 2003):16.

Gerding, Stephanie K., and Pamela H. MacKellar. *Library Grants* (blog). http://librarygrants .blogspot.com.

Giles, William. *Foundation Directory: Part 2.* 23rd ed. New York: Foundation Center, 2014.

Grants.gov. www.grants.gov.

Grantsmanship Center, The. www.tgci.com.

———. "Funding State-by-State." www.tgci.com/funding-sources.

GuideStar. www.guidestar.org.

Gutsche, Betha, and Brenda Hough, eds. *Competency Index for the Library Field.* Dublin, OH: OCLC Webjunction, 2014. www.webjunction.org/content/dam/WebJunction/ Documents/webJunction/2015-03/Competency%20Index%20for%20the%20 Library%20Field%20(2014).pdf.

Hall, Mary S., and Susan Howlett. *Getting Funded: The Complete Guide to Writing Grant Proposals.* 4th ed. Portland, OR: Portland State University, 2003.

Hall-Ellis, Sylvia D., and Ann Jerabek. *Grants for School Libraries.* Westport, CT: Libraries Unlimited, 2003.

Harris, Dianne. *The Complete Guide to Writing Effective and Award-Winning Grants: Step-by-Step Instructions.* Ocala, FL: Atlantic Publishers, 2007.

Henson, Kenneth T. *Successful Grant Writing for School Leaders: 10 Easy Steps.* Upper Saddle River, NJ: Pearson Education, 2011.

Idealware. *A Consumers Guide to Donor Management Systems*. Report by Idealware and NTEN, October 2013. www.idealware.org/reports/consumers-guide-donor -management-systems.

Information Today. *Annual Register of Grant Support: A Directory of Funding Sources*. New Medford, NJ: Information Today, annual.

———. *Corporate Giving Directory*. 37th ed. Medford, NJ: Information Today, 2015.

Institute of Museum and Library Services and Indiana University–Purdue University Indianapolis. "Shaping Outcomes." www.shapingoutcomes.org.

Landau, Herbert B. *Winning Library Grants: A Game Plan*. Chicago: American Library Association, 2011.

Leeder, Kim, and Eric Fierson. *Planning Our Future Libraries: Blueprints for 2025*. Chicago: American Library Association, 2014.

Legaspi, Nathan E. *A Government Guide to Grants*. New York: Nova Science Publishers, 2010.

Margolin, Judith B. *The Grantseeker's Guide to Winning Proposals*. New York: Foundation Center, 2008.

Maxwell, Nancy Kalikow, ed. *The ALA Book of Library Grant Money*. 9th ed. Chicago: American Library Association, 2014.

———. *Grant Money through Collaborative Partnerships*. Chicago: American Library Association, 2012.

McNamara, Carter. "A Basic Guide to Program Evaluation." Authenticity Consulting LLC, 2002. www.tgci.com/sites/default/files/pdf/A%20Basic%20Guide%20to%20 Program%20Evaluation_0.pdf.

Michigan State University Libraries. "Grants and Related Resources." Last revised January 23, 2015. http://staff.lib.msu.edu/harris23/grants.

Miller, Patrick W. *Grant-Writing: Strategies for Developing Winning Proposals*. 2nd ed. Munster, IN: Patrick W. Miller and Associates, 2002.

Miner, Jeremy T., and Lynn E. Miller. *Proposal Planning and Writing*. Westport, CT: Greenwood Press, 2008.

Nelson, Sandra S. *Implementing for Results: Your Strategic Plan in Action*. Chicago: Public Library Association, 2009.

———. *The New Planning for Results: A Streamlined Approach*. Chicago: Public Library Association, 2001.

———. *Strategic Planning for Results*. Chicago: Public Library Association, 2008.

Nelson, Sandra S., Ellen Altman, and Diane Mayo. *Managing for Results: Effective Resource Allocation for Public Libraries*. Chicago: Public Library Association, 2000.

New, Cheryl Carter, and James Aaron Quick. *How to Write a Grant Proposal*. Hoboken, NJ: John Wiley and Sons, 2003.

NOZAsearch. www.nozasearch.com.

OCLC. *From Awareness to Funding: A Study of Library Support in America*. Dublin, OH: OCLC, 2008. www.oclc.org/reports/funding.en.html.

Palgrave Macmillan. *Grants Register*. New York: Palgrave MacMillan, biennial.

Peterson, Susan Lee. *The Grantwriter's Internet Companion: A Resource for Educators and Others Seeking Grants and Funding*. San Francisco: Jossey-Bass, 2001.

Philanthropy News Digest. http://philanthropynewsdigest.org.

Public Library Association, Project Outcome. www.projectoutcome.org.

Quick, James Aaron, and Cheryl Carter New. *Grant Winner's Toolkit: Project Management and Evaluation*. New York: John Wiley and Sons, 2000.

Reif-Lehrer, Liane. *Grant Application Writer's Handbook.* 4th ed. Sudbury, MA: Jones and Bartlett, 2005.

Rosenfeld, Esther, and David V. Loertscher, eds. *Toward a 21st-Century School Library Media Program.* Lanham, MD: Scarecrow Press, 2007.

Smith, Nancy. *The Complete Book of Grant Writing: Learn to Write Grants Like a Professional.* Naperville, IL: Sourcebooks, 2012.

Smith, Nancy Burke, and Judy Tremore. *The Everything Grant Writing Book: Create the Perfect Proposal to Raise the Funds You Need.* 2nd ed. Cincinnati, OH: F+W Media, 2010.

Stains, Gail M. *Go Get That Grant! A Practical Guide for Libraries and Nonprofit Organizations.* Lanham, MD: Scarecrow Press, 2010.

TechSoup. "Choose the Right Donor Management Software through TechSoup: Find Out Which Tool Is Right for Your Organization." Posted October 17, 2014. www.techsoup.org/support/articles-and-how-tos/choose-the-right-donor -management-software-through-techsoup.

University of Washington Information School, IBEC (Information Behavior in Everyday Contexts). "Outcomes Toolkit Version 2.0." ibec.ischool.washington.edu/static/ ibeccat.aspx@subcat=outcome%20toolkit&cat=tools%20and%20resources.htm.

U.S. Census Bureau. www.census.gov.

———. American FactFinder. http://factfinder.census.gov.

———. "QuickFacts: United States." www.census.gov/quickfacts.

Ward, Deborah. *Writing Grant Proposals That Win.* Burlington, MA: Jones and Bartlett Learning, 2012.

Zilonis, Mary Frances, Carolyn Markuson, and Mary Beth Fincke. *Strategic Planning for School Library Media Centers.* Lanham, MD: Scarecrow Press, 2002.

About the Authors

Stephanie Gerding (www.stephaniegerding.com), MLIS, is a library consultant with twenty years of experience supporting libraries and nonprofits. Stephanie has success in all areas of grant work as a reviewer, writer, trainer, project manager, and consultant. She has been a lead grant reviewer of LSTA grants, state grants, and scholarships at the Arizona State Library and New Mexico State Library, and she has reviewed grants and serves as an advisor for the Bill & Melinda Gates Foundation. She has been awarded national grants and has been a program coordinator for many grant-funded projects. Recent projects include project management for the IMLS/Gates grant-funded Continuing Education Connector project led by the Chief Officers of State Libraries (COSLA); evaluation of the LSTA-funded Infopeople Eureka! Leadership program; training needs assessments for state and national organizations. She is a trainer for the PLA's national advocacy project, Turning the Page 2.0, Project Outcome, and developed the 2016 Dynamic Planning Institute. She has done consulting and training with TechSoup, PLA, and the Urban Libraries Council on the library technology benchmarking Edge Initiative. Stephanie leads webinars and online courses through Infopeople, PLA, NEFLIN (Northeast Florida Library Information Network), PCI Webinars, and other library organizations. She is a board member for ALA's Learning Round Table. Stephanie is an author of three books, including *Winning Grants* and *The Accidental Technology Trainer*. She lives in Seattle, Washington, with her husband and energetic eight-year-old daughter.

◇◇◇◇◇◇◇◇◇◇◇◇◇◇◇◇◇

Pamela H. MacKellar (www.pamelamackellar.com) is an author and library consultant who has worked in the library science field for over thirty years. Since earning a master's degree in library science from the State University of New York at Albany, she has held positions as a newspaper librarian, library director, assistant librarian, health sciences librarian, cataloger, technology consultant, and independent consultant in libraries of all kinds, including special, school, public, postsecondary, tribal, prison, and state.

Author of *Meeting Community Needs: A Practical Guide for Librarians* (Rowman & Littlefield, 2016), *Writing Successful Technology Grant Proposals: A LITA Guide* (Neal-Schuman, 2012) and *The Accidental Librarian* (Information Today, 2008), Pam has also co-written *Winning Grants: A How-To-Do-It Manual for Librarians with Multimedia Tutorials and Grant Development Tools* (Neal-Schuman, 2010) and *Grants for Libraries:*

A How-To-Do-It Manual (Neal-Schuman, 2006). She has written numerous articles, conducted workshops, and presented at many library conferences.

Pam has designed and taught online courses and workshops on grants for libraries and nonprofits; written successful proposals for government and foundation grants; planned and administered grant projects; and reviewed grant proposals for federal and state agencies. She was the recipient of the 2010 Loleta D. Fyan Award from the American Library Association for an "Online Management Course for New Library Directors in New Mexico."

In addition, Pam designs and creates websites for small public libraries. She is also a printmaker, makes artist books, and teaches book arts classes (www.pamonpaper .com). Pam lives in New Mexico with her husband and two cats.

Index